A LIGHT IN AFRICA

LYNN KAZIAH GISSING

known as

MAMA LYNN

FOUNDER OF THE NGO LIGHT IN AFRICA
CHILDREN'S HOMES, TANZANIA, EAST AFRICA

LEADERS IN GLOBAL PUBLISHING

Published by Motivational Press, Inc.
7777 N Wickham Rd, # 12-247
Melbourne, FL 32940
www.MotivationalPress.com

Manufactured in the United States of America.

ISBN: 978-1-62865-073-0

Contents

DEDICATION

This book is dedicated firstly to the God whom I serve who trusted me to love and care for His 'treasures' on earth. This is my third generation of child rearing, and this book is dedicated not only to my children whom I have raised, my grandchildren and great grandchildren, but also to all the children who has touched my life and all the 'precious' children of Light in Africa. This book has been written especially for you so that you can know just how much God loves you. God Bless you all.

FORWARD

I believe in a God Who performs miracles, but this God could never use me. I am just a middle class, middle-aged English-woman, with no money, power, or political connections. "No God, not me!"

That could have been Lynn Gissing's reaction in 1999 when she heard a voice in her head telling her to "Go to Africa." She could have said, "No God, not me!" Instead, she walked forward in a step of faith and trust. This book tells the story of what happened next, because of one woman's "Yes, God."

We first heard of "Mama Lynn," as Lynn Gissing is known to everybody, in 2005 when our Malibu, CA preschool began a search for a "sister school" to help our young children and their parents expand their worldview. One of our former preschool children had completed a Social Work Internship at a place called "Light in Africa" in Moshi, Tanzania. It was founded by a remarkable Englishwoman who as a policy never asked for money or outside support. Instead, she took her requests to God, and then waited on Him. Intrigued, we made the connection, and a friendship was formed.

Over the past nine years, we have traveled to Light in Africa to see for ourselves what God is doing there, and Mama Lynn has been a guest in our home several times. We have laughed and swapped stories with this witty, energetic, servant of Jesus on our deck overlooking the Pacific Ocean. Mama Lynn has enjoyed a glass or two of sweet white wine, some well done beef, a sweet or two, American reality TV, and many, many cups of tea with us. But we also have witnessed her wrestling with God as to where He is leading her, and Light in Africa, next. It is an honor and a privilege to be a small part of this great ministry.

We truly believe that our great God brought Mama Lynn to Africa "for such a time as this" (Esther 4:14). As you read her story, we pray that your hearts will be touched, as you grasp how wide and long and high and deep the love of God is for all His children. Read, pray, listen to God's voice, and respond. You will be blessed.

Cindy and Jim Ludwig
Malibu Presbyterian Nursery School
Malibu, CA, USA
September 30, 2013

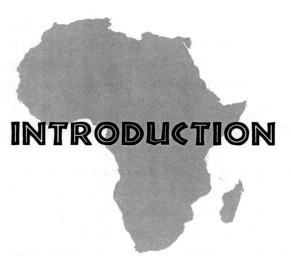

INTRODUCTION

This book is very simply written, because I am a very plain and simple person, but I have one thing going for me that places everything I do into perspective and that is "Jesus Loves Me".

This true story that I have written about is how, one day, at fifty five years of age, a mature English women, with a comfortable life-style was clearly instructed by a higher power to "Go To Africa", and how fourteen years later the consequences of following those instructions given in 1999 have resulted in thousands of people being helped and many lives being saved, sometimes in the most miraculous of ways.

In June 2000, I boarded an airplane and landed at Kilimanjaro International Airport in Tanzania, East Africa, not knowing what life had in store for me due to this immeasurable decision that I had made – which was considered by my family to be 'utterly crazy and irresponsible'" - to sell everything that I owned and to go to live in Tanzania, and to try to help those suffering children who had no-one to love or care for them whilst they died of the HIV/AIDS virus, or whether this decision was to be the biggest mistake that I had ever made in my life.

Within six weeks of my arrival in the country, I had found a dere-lict building that was located 6,000 feet up on the foothills of Mount

Kilimanjaro which would be suitable for the first children's home. However, even before one child came into care, I had started to respond to the needs of the local Chagga tribe by operating the first weekly out-reach food program. Due to to the immense needs of the poor, a weekly out-reach medical dispensary followed, then the children started to arrive.

I had brought with me all my core values that I believed in but I was soon to realize that this different culture didn't operate on the same wave-length that I had known, therefore many mistakes were made and much 'soul searching' was done to allow me to adapt to this new mountain life environment.

I have been blessed over these last fourteen years to have been allowed to witness 'my first fruits' of my endeavors in so much as the children that I took from off the streets and the children who were starving and not expected to survive are now in their twenties and are studying in collages in Dar es Salaam. One is to be a teacher, one a social worker, one a business administrator, and one is to become a doctor.

Other blessings that I unexpectedly received whilst on this journey were two of my adult children along with my grandchildren coming over to Tanzania to help me with this mission.

Marcus, my youngest son, a strong 'prayer warrior,' and my staunchest ally and supporter, convinced me to find the time to write this book to document the history and the super-natural interventions that have occurred for the spiritual enlightenment of the past, present and future children of our NGO Light in Africa Children's Homes. This true record of my time living in Tanzania I humbly submit for your reading. All the names of the children in this book have been changed for confidentiality reasons, and also the people that I have been involved with, except for those who have kindly granted me permission to use their rightful names.

I pray, dear reader, that you will be inspired by this book to be a light and a blessing to someone who is in need and to not shirk from offering a helping hand of friendship and support. Yes, I agree it can come at a cost to your comfort zone, but the benefits far out weigh the inconveniences, and who knows, you may even be blessed in receiving hundreds of bountiful treasures the same as I, and all I did was to believe, by faith, that it was better to give than to receive and the treasure arrived on my doorstep.

Then Peter spoke up. "Look, we have left everything and followed you". "Yes", Jesus said to them, "and I tell you that those who leave home or brothers or sisters, or mother or father or children or fields for me and for the gospel, will receive much more in this present age. They will receive a hundred times more houses, brothers, sisters, mothers , children and fields – and persecutions as well"

Mark 10 v 28. (Good News Bible)

I have indeed been blessed with many homes, many brothers to work with, many sisters to spend time and to share with, many mothers to help and support who had no one they could turn to in their times of need, many fathers whom I have cared for either with housing or medical support, hundreds of children to love and to care for and many fields to grow our crops in.

The persecutions that I had to endure seemed insurmountable at the time but quite essential for me in building faith and dependence on God through prayer.

For many month's, I kept receiving one word and that word was "diluted". My church is being "diluted". How has it happened that the Lord's Prayer is no longer spoken in assembly's or any Christian worship is allowed in overseas' Government schools. People are fearful even to say that they believe in an Awesome God. How have we just stood back as Christian believers and done nothing and allowed our faith to be trampled on and diluted? We have the power of the Holy Spirit to move mountains, so why aren't we? "For God did not give us a spirit of timidity but a spirit of power, of love and of self-discipline." (NIV Study Bible)

Wouldn't it be a wonderful thing if we could have a global day where the world comes together as one to pray for world peace, starvation, medical cures, global warming, etc., together in prayer we could make a huge difference to our planet that we call home.

Abundant blessing to each and every one.

Mama Lynn
Founder of Light in Africa Children's Homes.
Alias Lynn Kaziah Gissing.

CHAPTER ONE
TRUE LOVE

The young man paced up and down the hospital waiting room floor, anxious and distressed, his heart feeling uncontrollable sadness. Only a few hours earlier he had been called into his employer's office to be told that his long-time girlfriend had been involved in a serious accident and he was urgently needed at the hospital. On enquiring about her condition, he was told nothing. All the many nurses he had asked for information had all given the same frustrating answer: "Please wait" and "the surgeon will be with you shortly". The hours ticked by and people came into the waiting room and left to visit their 'loved ones' but he still had no news about his Ellen.

They had met a few years earlier and straight away 'hit it off.'

They both loved going out into the countryside on his motorbike, and she was always there to 'cheer' him on at the many shows where he used to perform stunts on his motorbike; from going round and round on the 'wheel of death' to jumping though 'hoops of fire,' Ellen was always there.

Ellen was an orphan and had been given away at birth to a disabled lady to bring up. She always made sure that 'mam' had everything she needed before she left the house to accompany William to the showground. "Ellen really has a sweet, caring nature, he mused. Instinctively, he heard heavier footsteps coming down the corridor and looked towards the heavy brass door handle as the footsteps stopped outside of the waiting room. He rose to his feet as the door opened and a grey haired gentleman with a handlebar moustache wearing a white coat walked into the room. "William Gissing is it?" the doctor asked as he held out his hand to shake the young man's hand. "Yes" William replied. "The news is not good I'm afraid", the surgeon said quietly. The next few hours are critical to her survival. Her back was broken when she landed at the bottom of the lift shaft, and the trolley full of jam that she was pulling fell on top of her which has resulted in massive internal injuries and bruising." The doctor waited a moment for the news to sink in to the young man's consciousness. He then went over and took a chair and placed it in front of the one William had been sitting on. "Please sit down. I have something I would like to say to you." William sat down obediently, his mind unable to accept that before the day was out his Ellen could be dead. "What I am about to say may seem a little harsh to you" said the doctor, "but I assure you, I have the very best interest and your welfare at heart. Ellen is in a very serious condition, and she probably won't survive this accident. If she does, she will be a 'cripple' for the rest of her life. She will never be able to walk again, will never be able to bear you any children, and will always need assistance with the most 'basic' of functions. The very best thing that I can advise and recommend that you to do is to leave this hospital right now and not come back. Just leave and start a new life. It's for the very best, I assure you." Shocked at the news and trying to hold back the dam of emotions that was threatening to break, he stared down at his darkened black fingernails which still contained diesel oil from the engine he had been repairing before his boss called him into his office.

The doctor patiently waited until the young man had fully digested this information that he had just given him. William lifted his head to look the doctor straight into his eyes and said, "If I had been injured in an accident at work or had fallen off my motorcycle at the showground, I know that Ellen would never just get up and leave me. She would lovingly care for all of my needs no matter what they were. I'm not going to leave her now that she needs me. We'll get through this, because we have faith," and quickly the young man stood up, shook the doctor's hand and thanked him for all that he had done for 'his Ellen.' He opened the door and hurried out of the room, found the gents toilet, bolted the door, and broke into heart wrenching sobs.

This story is about my mother and father, the stock that I come from. The love, courage, strength and resilience that they both showed that terrible day when my mother responded to a call for help in pulling a cart full of newly made jam to a lift to take it to the ground floor of the jam factory where she worked in the office. Unfortunately, the lift was not there as she stepped backwards and she fell to the bottom of the shaft pulling the trolley on top of her as she fell.

My father encouraged my mother to walk again by making her two promises. The first promise was that the day that she could get off the water bed that she had lain on for six months and stand in front of him, unaided, was the day he would slip an engagement ring on her finger. The second was that the day that she walked down the hospital corridor to meet him when he visited her would be the day they would plan their wedding day.

Even though it was to take many months of sheer pain and determination, my mother did eventually make the long walk down the hospital corridor and she married my father encased in Plaster of Paris from her neck to her thighs.

To my mind, this is a 'classic' love story. Contrary to the doctor's diagnoses, my mother did walk unaided and presented my father with four children. One infant died, and I was the last to be born. My father passed away at the age of eighty three years and mother at the grand age of one hundred and two years.

During the second world war, my father, William Henry Livingstone Gissing (always ready to tell a good yarn to anyone who would listen) was heavily involved in repairing and maintaining the diesel engines of the many ships that docked at the port of Grimsby where we lived. On one occasion – as the story goes – a destroyer had moored outside the harbour limits with a serious problem that the ship's apparatus, which throws "depth charges" overboard into the sea to explode at a certain depth and sink enemy submarines, had failed to release one of the explosive barrels and throw it from the rear of the ship. It was now hanging very precariously – neither in nor out – of its holding mechanism. Any sudden movement of the ship could dislodge the barrel, and it would 'plop' overboard and blow up the ship.

My father was asked to board the ship and see if he could repair the holding mechanism system and return the lodged depth charge to its neutral position. He was also solemnly informed of the consequences of failure! As he was taken to the ship on a motor launch, he passed all of the ships personnel being evacuated. I'm sure quite a sobering thought of what could happen to him in the next few hours if he failed to complete the mission and disengage the depth charge. Thankfully, he successfully repaired the mechanism, and everyone could breath safely again.

My earliest memories were of being on boats! On a Sunday morning, my father would sit me on the seat he had welded for me on his bicycle, and we would cycle down to the docks. This, I clearly remember, was a time of special joy for me as a five year old. I would be carried over the seiners (fishing boats) sometimes ten ships deep, being passed over from one ship to another with a willing hands until I was carefully set down on the captains ship that we needed to visit and enjoy a 'cup of tea and biscuits' and very long conversations. The ride home would consist of me holding a large parcel of fresh fish wrapped in newspapers straddled across my lap and that would be our dinner for that evening.

Each November, I visit my 'home town' in the UK to speak at different engagements and one is lucky to see a handful of fishing boats tied to the wall as the majority of seiners have all been decommissioned.

Some pretty stoic, determined Christian people who have changed the course of English history have come from 'my neck of the woods' in Lincolnshire.

Twenty five miles away (as the crow flies), the famous slave abolitionist William Wilberforce (1759-1833) was born in Hull, Yorkshire. He was a politician who led the suppression of the slave trade through parliament. Epworth in the Isle of Axholme is where John Wesley, the Founding Father of Methodism, was born along with Charles, his brother. Susanna, their mother, gave birth to nineteen children, and when stressed by all the noise the children would make, she used to pull her long pinafore that was covering her dress over her head and start to pray. England's first female Prime Minister, Baroness Margaret Thatcher, was also born in Grantham, Lincolnshire, (1925 – 2013). Another notable figure born in the vicinity was Issac Newton (1643-1727), considered by some to be the greatest scientist ever to be born. Each one of these great people knew what the face of opposition looked like, but their courage and desire to make the world a better place was their guiding principles.

We had our own small boat called the 'Dorothy', and the family would enter into the spirit of the yachting community enjoying the many regatta's, and on the day of the presentation of the cups that had been won by different classes, I was allowed to go to school with my hair in metal curlers and rags to make ringlets. What a frightful sight I must have looked but I didn't care because I had a new dress waiting to be put on at home, and I would be able to stay up late that night. Happy memories, but all was about to change when my father bought an ailing garage and petrol station in the countryside.

My older sister and brother were already grown up and working, so for a six year old starting a new village school, it was quite a daunting prospect.

The biggest thing that I noticed in my little life was that there was no more 'family time' or going down to the boat to play, as now all that my parents ever seemed to do was work. The beloved 'Dorothy' was sold, and it was nothing but the garage and the petrol pumps for me for the following twelve years.

As my father was a very good mechanic but a hopeless business-man it fell to me to prepare all the accounts for the auditors beginning when I was eleven years of age. In recollection, I can only remember one occasion that both my parents accompanied me on an outing in the car, and that was to take me to the hospital as I had been diag-nosed with meningitis!

But one thing my father always did every single night no matter how late he had been working in the garage and that was to come into my bedroom, tuck the sheets in tightly around the bed, kiss my fore-head, and say; "Goodnight darling, I love you, sleep tight and don't forget to say your prayers."

CHAPTER TWO
JEHOVAH JIRAH MY PROVIDER

An early marriage, which expanded my geography of the UK as we travelled around the country for my husband's work, resulted in my three children all being born in different counties. At three years of age, my daughter was diagnosed with a heart murmur (Pulmonary Stenosis) and was booked into a Children's hospital for heart surgery. As we lived quite a distance away from the hospital, I was allowed to stay at the hospital with her. Each Wednesday, a child would undergo heart surgery, and as I was still in the wards reading stories and playing with the children long after their parents and visitors had left, I became very friendly with the children and knew them all by name. When Wednesday came around, Julian, a three year old little boy, went down to the operating theatre for his operation, and I prayed that his little blue lips and his blue fingertips would be a lovely puce colour after the operation, but sadly, this was not to be. Julian died on the operating table. I was saddened to watch floral tributes arrive at the sister's nursing station.

It was now Tuesday evening, and my daughters heart operation was scheduled for the following day, when this young nurse came over to me and suggested that I run a bubble bath for her and spend time playing with my child. It was how the nurse had said it that sent 'shock waves' through my system. "She thinks she might die tomorrow and she wants me to spend some last 'happy time' with her," I thought. I left the ward and went to my allotted bedroom at the hospital to pray. Filled with anxiety, I couldn't comprehend that by the next day I might not have a beautiful little girl to love and to cherish. What could I do? Should I stop the operation going ahead? The doctors had fully explained to me that, without the chance of an operation, she would not live to the age of five, but of course, there were no promises or guarantees that the operation would be a success either, as she was a very seriously sick little girl. After some time alone, I knew what I had to do. It was 8:00 p.m. when I went to tell the nursing sister that I had to have a hospital chaplain come and pray over my daughter before the operation. "It is too late to ask the chaplain to come" she responded. "Then the operation cannot go ahead until he does come," I answered back and walked away to the dimly lit ward to stare at my daughter soundly sleeping in her bed. At 11:15 p.m. a nurse walked quietly down the center of the ward and came to the bedside. "The hospital Chaplain is here now if you would like to see him in the sister's office," she said and walked away. I woke my daughter and, still half asleep, she nestled into the crook of my neck as I carried her to the night sister's office.

My first reaction to the young man in his late twenties was one of surprise, as for some reason I expected to meet with a much older man. He greeted me warmly and asked me to explain the situation to him which I did. "Before the operation takes place tomorrow" I said, "I need to be re-assured by prayer that she is safe in the arms of Jesus being taken care of no matter what the outcome will be." The Chaplain nodded his head as he rested his hand gently on the top of her head as she sat quietly on my knee. The lengthy prayer caused me to think that this young man has power in his prayers, filled me with a peace to accept whatever the outcome would be. I couldn't humanly do any more except to commit her into the arms of Jesus for Him to take great care of her whilst she underwent this major surgery and that the hands and minds of the many doctors and nurses which would be present with her would have the peace that passeth all understanding during the operation.

The following day, as the nurses prepared her for the operation, I calmly let her be wheeled away to the theatre, and I went to my room to pray. The operation took many hours. A nurse knocked on my door to inform me the operation was now over and she had been taken to the intensive care room. I hurried down the corridor anxious to see her and was shocked when I entered the room to see my little girl on this large bed with pipes and machinery adorning her. A nurse pulled up a chair for me to sit on, and all of a sudden she sat straight up in bed, transfixed. I let out a cry of anguish. "It's a reaction to the anesthetic," the nurse explained as she gently laid the child back down on the bed. "I think perhaps you should leave her now and go to the canteen and get yourself something to eat. I will call you if there are any changes to her medical condition," said this kind nurse. I placed the chair back to its original position and left the room. With the help of the physiotherapy department, who was massaging her little chest many times throughout the day and night for fear of pneumonia setting in, she was eventually returned to the ward having been stapled and stitched from the top of her chest to her waist. Days later, my parents came to the hospital to visit, and I remember my mother bursting into tears as she saw her youngest granddaughter walking down the corridor all hunched up with the tightness of the stitches like a little old women.

The following Wednesday another heart operation was carried out on a seven year old boy, and sadly, he too did not recover from the surgery.

By the age of thirty, I was divorced with three young children to nurture on my own. That was really the start of my dependence on God for His provision in our lives. Money was scarce, and each Saturday my parents would take the children shopping and bring back a large box of food which would tie me over until the following Tuesday when I could collect our weekly government benefits.

One day, our pantry was bare. Like Mother Hubbard, I had nothing in the cupboard for the children's evening meal when they returned home from school. I went upstairs to my bedroom to pray. "Lord, you know I have no food to give my children for dinner this evening. In your word, You say that you know my needs before I have even asked. Please help me now to find the money to purchase food for dinner this evening."

I returned downstairs, thinking about all of my options. There were still a couple of hours before the children would be home. I heard a noise outside like a large hissing sound, and a vehicle pulled up outside the cottage where we lived. My brother jumped out of the cab and came to the back door; as he had had a puncture in his lorry. I automatically went to put the kettle on whilst he went back to change the tyre. After drinking his cup of tea, he handed me a five pound note and left. I hurriedly put on my coat and went to the nearest shops to purchase meat and vegetables, and a cooked dinner was ready for when the children returned home from school.

Wherever I have lived, I have always attended a nearby church. This dependence on God for all of my needs has always been a strong force in my life. Jehovah Jirah has never failed to provide for me through prayer, and I was later to place an altogether larger prospect before Him other than my three children's needs.

Years later, I re-married, and as the children moved onto higher education I was employed by the local authorities, first as a Deaf/Blind Guide, and then as a Social Worker with the Deaf/Interpreter. I held this position, until one day as I was driving along the motorway, I suddenly experienced an excruciating pain in the back of my neck. A visit to the hospital diagnosed an eroded disc caused by my hands and arms always being in motion with all the interpreting, communicating, and driving that I was employed to do. I enjoyed using my hands to marry profoundly deaf people, bury them, interpret for the police, courts, doctors, or any other situation where the voice of a deaf person needed to be heard through the interpretation of sign language, but due to my health, this could no longer be my job. I was pensioned off from work, sold the renovated tudor-style cottage with an acre of land where we had lived whilst the children were growing up and then moved onto a converted seiner (fishing boat) for the next three years until we moved back into the property market and became Foster Carers.

At times my, home looked as if World War III had broken out as we accommodated children who had some pretty severe behavioral problems. On school days from 1:30 p.m. to 3:00 p.m. I could usually be found taking spiritual refreshment in the local Christian bookshop, which provided a haven of peace and quiet where I could just sit and read a book, watch a video on a 'hero of the faith,' or just enjoy a cup of tea before it was time for me to collect the children from school when my role would change, and I would become a referee or a peacemaker.

We fostered children for many years, and it was always a particular joy to see the advances in confidence the children would make as soon as they felt they were living in a safe and secure environment and that we had the time to listen and care about their needs.

On an impulse one day, I decided to place our home on the market for sale and purchase some property in the country. I had enquired on the potential of the sale and was told it would probably take around eighteen months as the property market was in a trough and that was how long it was taking for the houses to be sold down the avenue where we lived. Amazingly, just the same as when I had placed the cottage on the market, a potential buyer was found three days after the signboard was erected. With the contract signed and the furniture stored around the families homes, I made the decision that it was now going to be 'my time' after years of always being busy and on the go. I was going to spend the three months of winter on the Algarve in Portugal.

CHAPTER THREE
SPIRITUAL AWAKENING

I arrived at the 'low season' hotel and quickly made a program of action. After breakfast each morning, I would walk down to the beach, sit on a rock, watch the perpetual movement of the tide come in and go out and enjoy watching the fishermen cleaning their brightly painted boats. They had been pulled out of the water onto the beach to enable the seaweed and fishguts to be removed from their preveious nights fishing for shoals of sardines. The fishermen, with cigarettes hanging out of their mouths would gather together, three or four men in a group, sit on upturned lobster pots, and with nimble fingers, busily repairing their holey fishing nets as they nattered away, possibly like so many fishermen that I knew always talking about 'the one that got away'.

I had promised myself that I would read 'without disturbance' the many popular Christian books that I never seemed to have time to fully read and once again started to read the Bible from cover to cover.

On my first Sunday in Portugal, I walked into town and found a tourist church which held the service in English and not in Portuguese. The Pastor of the church was a missionary from the United States.

I was also introduced to a young missionary called Daniel from the UK who had come to live with his young family on the Algarve.

An arrangement was made where, each Sunday, Daniel would collect me from the hotel and take me and other tourists to different English speaking churches. On one particular Sunday, after the service had started and we had sung praises to the Lord, I received my very first 'mind's eye' picture that came into focus and has been part of my spiritual life ever since.

As I stared I, could see a very clear scene of a river bank, and then I could see to the bottom of the river – rather like looking into an aquarium - I could see the grit and sand particles at the bottom, the swaying green weeds as they drifted lazily with the current, and it looked quite a serene picture. Then suddenly, I saw a speedboat moving at high speed across the picture and creating a heavy wash, and then all the sediment of the riverbed was swirled around so that every particle was changed and disturbed. Then the words to accompany the 'picture' came into my mind. "This church is going to be stirred up." Later after the service, I explained to the Pastor the picture that I had seen in my 'mind's eye'. After I had left Portugal, I received a letter from Daniel informing me that the church had been so 'stirred up' to the point of nearly closing down.

The second picture that I received after a time of contemplation and meditation, happened in the middle of the night. I was awakened for whatever reason I cannot now remember, but when I opened my eyes I could see a 'sumptuous' rich fruit cake. As I looked at the cake, it started to cover itself with yellow marzipan, and then it covered itself with white icing, and then it was decorated like a wedding cake. The words that followed were for the mature US American Pastor of the first church that I had attended. God was happy with this mature faithful servant (fruit cake) but he wanted to give him much more spiritual gifts (marzipan, icing) than he already had. I fell back to sleep and the following day spoke to an English Pastor as to what it could all possibly mean. 'Two years previously' he said, another visitor to his church had had the very same 'wedding picture' that I had just described, on that occasion it was for a member of his congregation.

As seeing moving pictures in my 'mind's eye' was something new to me, the Pastor encouraged me to always pass on the 'picture' for whom it was intended , and advised me that I must always 'follow through' and give it to the person God intended it for, whether it was a 'good' picture or a not so good picture. I might not know the intention behind it, but it might have a significant meaning to the receiver of the picture, something perhaps that they had been earnestly praying for, or some revelation. I agreed that the following Sunday I would pass the 'mind picture' that I had seen on to the American Pastor.

Sunday arrived, and I caught the bus into town. I sat by a window seat and started to stare out of the window. A motorcycle drew alongside intending to overtake the bus. The driver was in full black leather motorbike gear, as was his passenger who was holding on tightly with arms wrapped around the driver. The words came, "We are going to go on a long journey, and all that I ask of you is to hold on to me firmly as I know the road that we are going to travel," and the motorcycle revved up and pulled away and overtook the bus. "What was that all about." I thought and on my return to the hotel wrote it all down in my journal.

I did as the Pastor had recommended and gave the picture information of the 'fruit cake' on to the tourist Pastor, and I returned home.

One afternoon, as I walked along the beach picking up and admiring the many shells that were washed up on the shore line, I started to hear the sound of a dog incessantly barking high up on the cliff tops. "Something's wrong with the dog," I thought. "I should just go and take a look to see if it is trapped or in some sort of trouble." I walked across the sand to the bottom step and looked up at the high climb that I would have to navigate to reach the top of the cliff and wondered if it was worth the effort, but the dog was still barking so I considered the exercise would be good for me and started the steep climb trying to stay as closely as I could to the side of the cliff. Panting heavily from the excursion, I eventually reached the top to see the barking dog was actually stuck up a tree on a low hanging branch.

How it had managed to jump up on to the branch I had no idea but there it was barking away. What strange and bizarre behavior the dog was exhibiting. Why was it going crazy like this? I walked over to the security barrier and looked over the cliff top towards the Mediterranean Sea; it certainly was a stunning view. I slowly turned around again to watch the dog, and that's when I saw it. High up on the top most branch of the tree, sat washing himself without a care in the world the largest marmalade cat that I had ever seen. So this is what the dog was going hypo for! A cat! I watched the cat washing his face first with one paw and then with another and the words of a hymn came floating into my mind.

> Blessed assurance Jesus is mine
>
> Oh what a foretaste of glory divine!
>
> Heir of salvation, purchase of God;
>
> Born of his Spirit, washed in his blood;
>
> Chorus   This is my story, this is my song,
>
> Praising my Saviour all the day long.
>
> *(Frances Jane van Alstyne 1820-1915)*

And the words that followed: "No matter the danger or the situation, remember this: be like this cat, totally assured that you are resting and safe in the arms of Jesus."

It was a Saturday afternoon, and the wind was howling around the skyscraper hotel making a lot of noise. It was pretty obvious that a storm was brewing out at sea, and it would not be too long before it hit the coastline. I was in the bedroom of my hotel room on the fifth floor sitting on my bed counting out the money that I had in my purse to ensure that I had sufficient for my tithe the following day. As I handled the money, I had a sense that I was not to give the money to the church as a tithe. Twenty minutes later, I sensed another message and that was that I had to go into town to the ATM machine and draw some more money out. I went over to the window and looked out at the darkened sky, wondered if should I risk it or not?" If the weather really gets bad I thought I suppose I could always return to the hotel in a taxi."

As I passed through the foyer of the hotel, the wind hit me straight in my face. I battled against it for the following thirty minutes whilst I walked in to town. I really didn't know what I was supposed to do or how much Portuguese money I was supposed to take out of the ATM as I put my pin number into the machine and I just stared at the numbers. "Oh well, I don't understand any of this, I suppose I'm just making a fool of myself," and I pressed a number on the key pad. The familiar sound of money being counted could be heard as I waited for it to be dispatched through the aperture.

I took the money and placed it in my purse, and decided to stop at a coffee shop for a coffee and a pastry. On my return to the hotel, I found a full-length plate glass window in the foyer had been smashed to smithereens by the wind. Slivers and large pieces of glass were scattered over a large area of the foyer, and the hotel staff tried to negotiate the guests around the glass on the floor whilst the sweeping up operations were underway. Thankfully, no one was walking by at the time of the accident or else it could have been a very serious situation with glass flying everywhere. I was pleased that I had decided to go to a coffee shop and have a drink before I had returned to the hotel. I skirted the debris and took the lift up to my floor. As I sat on the bed once again a third message came into my mind, and told me that I had to place all of the money, including the tithing money, into an envelope and give the envelope to Daniel in the morning.

As I waited by the hotel steps for the vehicle to arrive to take me over the river to a different church, I considered all the things that had happened to me since I made the decision to take some 'time out'. With plenty of time on my hands to please myself I was feeling more relaxed, more contented, than I had ever felt in a long time, and I felt closer to God than I could ever remember. His word had more meaning now that I had the time to meditate upon it.

Daniel pulled up outside the hotel, and he opened the door for me to get into the car. I strapped myself into the front seat, and I then handed Daniel the envelope out of my bag, saying 'I was just told to give you this'. He placed the envelope into his jacket pocket and we drove off. After the service, Daniel asked if I would like to attend an evening service at another church he was going to attend. Not one to miss a chance to Praise the Lord, I readily agreed.

As the Pastor completed his evening sermon, Daniel stood up to speak to the congregation. He said, "I want to share something with you this evening that happened today. This morning I was handed an envelope which, when I opened it, contained money. What the person who gave me the envelope doesn't know is that my wife and I have been earnestly praying all week to receive funds to pay our telephone bill as it was going to be 'cut-off' on Monday, and when I counted the money there was the exact amount of money to pay the bill. Jesus certainly hears the prayers of his people". So that was what it was all about! All that had been asked of me was to listen to the 'small quiet voice' and to act and not to dismiss it as my wild imagination or insignificant murmurings. I was now on 'spiritual fire' for God, and I must have been a real 'pain' to the people whom I met, as I wanted to share this new gift that I had been given with everyone. I was seeing and feeling things for the first time in a completely different yet much clearer way, and even the sky looked more magnificent than I could ever remember it looking before. It was all so exciting.

With my three months holiday now over, I caught the airplane back to the UK, but I wasn't ready to start looking for a new house to live in. I wanted to experience much more of the Holy Spirit, and I was eager for whatever God wanted to give to me, so I re-packed all of my suitcases, jumped into my car, drove down to Plymouth, caught the ferry to Santander, and drove all the way through Spain back to the Algarve where I stayed a further three months making a total of six months break from everyday life.

CHAPTER FOUR
THE COMMISSION

It was now May of 1999, and all the trees and flowers were looking splendid as I returned to the UK. As I had nowhere to live, I bought a caravan and placed it on a camping site, which amongst its facilities had a lovely indoor swimming pool and gym.

I was now intent on finding a house in the country to live in, and one of the prerequisites was that it had to have some land so I could once again enjoy my hobby of gardening. It was a market day in Louth, Lincolnshire, and I thought I would visit the town and collect some property brochures of some of the area's properties that were on the market for sale. I parked the car and started to walk down the side street when all of a sudden I heard quite clearly in my mind the words: "Go to Africa." "How very strange," I thought "Where did that thought come from. I'm thinking of what to buy for dinner: pork chops, pork sausages or a pork pie". I continued walking down the street, my mind moving on to other things. Then again the voice in my head said, "Go to Africa." This time the voice was clearer and more concise. I looked around to see if I could see a camera crew, thinking perhaps I was being 'set up" for something like Candid Camera wanting to make a fool out of me. I thought I'd best hurry along to the main street, as there is always safety in numbers. I walked into the main shopping area where all the stalls were laid out with their goods on display for sale. This small market town felt comfortable and welcoming. I think it would be quite nice to live around this area and get involved in something, like perhaps a gardening club or an evening class and learn a new skill like IT that everyone was talking about. My oldest independent son was suggesting that I should buy a computer and have an email address, whatever that was.

I carried on walking down the main street, when quite suddenly I became stuck to the pavement; literally. My feet couldn't and wouldn't move. I'm stood like a statue, rooted to the spot. I tried to move my feet again, but I couldn't. Panic sets in, "Oh dear God, am I having a medical stroke?" I tried to move my feet again, but I couldn't move my shoes even an inch. As I stood in the middle of the pavement with people passing me by on either side, I hear that voice again: "Go into the travel agency and book a ticket to Africa". "What ?!" I scream in my mind. I look to the left of me where all of the shops are situated and there, on my left side, is a travel agency which I hadn't noticed before. I tried to move my feet again, but I'm definitely stuck to the spot. With people staring at me as they pass by, I start to try to make some sense of this situation. I recalled all that had happened to me in Portugal, and the fact that I didn't baulk at those experiences. Instead, I found it thrilling and exciting that the Deity had 'tested' me to see if I would obey the mind instructions that had been given to me, but this was something totally extreme. "Go to Africa" Where was Africa anyway? How long I stood in that one position I have no way of knowing. I tried to think this through logically before I was totally consumed by panic. I had attended churches for over forty odd years but always as a member of a congregation. I hadn't even attended any theology courses. "Why had God asked such a sinful person like me to 'Go to Africa?' Had there been someone else in the Bible who couldn't believe that God would ask them to do something for Him? No sooner had the thought occurred than Gideon came to my mind. In the Old Testament in Judges 6:36, Gideon cannot believe that God would ask him, the youngest of his family, to help save Israel from the Midianites and lead an army against them, so he did what any sane person would do. He laid down a sheep's skin and said to God, "God if this is really you speaking with me; tonight I want the sheepskin to be full of dew and the ground dry." God did what was asked of Him and Gideon was able to ring out a bowl of water from the fleece. He then asked God to do one more thing with the fleece. "Tonight" he said, "I want the sheepskin to be dry and the ground wet with dew." And God answered that request too. Gideon, now knowing that God was with him, won the war with just 300 soldiers instead of a vast army. All these thoughts passed through my mind as I was still 'glued' to the pavement. "OK God, this is my fleece. Just like Gideon asked you for confirmation, I am asking too. If you want me to go to Africa, then my fleece will be this; I will go into that travel agency and if within ten minutes I have a ticket to go to Africa, then I will go. No ticket within ten minutes, then I know I am either having a mid-life crisis, or a mental breakdown, or I urgently need to speak to a psychologist about the 'voices' I'm hearing in my mind. I could even be seriously sick and not know it!"

This time, when I tried to move, I did. My feet were free to move, and I walked straight over to the travel agency door, opened it, walked in, and went over to the chair closest to the desk where a lady was busy on her computer. "Good morning, madam," said the 'smiley' lady behind the desk, "how may I help you?" "I would like to go to Africa please," I responded. "Yes madam", the 'smiley' lady replied, "Africa is a very large continent. Where exactly would you like to go?" The lady was staring at me intently waiting for an answer. I screamed into my mind, "God where am I going"? I continued to stare into her 'smiley' face and waited. Then in my mind I remembered that I had been writing to a Pastor in a place called Moshi in Tanzania, East Africa, for over six years. The church that I had been attending had a notice board in their coffee lounge advising the congregation that they were intending to fill a container with boxes of dried food as local Pastors where experiencing a difficult time due to a drought. Anyone interested in participating should cross a name off the list of thirty two Pastors names. I had just drawn a line through one of the names, filled a box, written a letter and enclosed it in the box, and sealed it up and the Pastor had responded back to my letter and we had communicated by air mail learning about each other's cultures. "Take me to the nearest airport to a place called Moshi in Tanzania please," I at last responded. The ladies hands flew over the keyboard, and she looked up and said, "Well madam, I have a very cheap ticket available for one month in November, shall I book it now?" "Yes please," I responded and completed all the necessary requirements. The door of the travel agency closed behind me, and I was once again standing upon the pavement, when reality 'hit'. "Oh my goodness! What have I just gone and done? What on earth will my family say to me about going to Africa by myself in November?!" Well, quite naturally, they did have quite a lot to say about my trip to Africa. And the concerns were expressed quite strongly right up to the time that I boarded the plane by myself in November 1999, but I knew deep within me that I would never have any peace of mind if I did not check out that burning question: Did God tell me to "GO TO AFRICA?"

I arrived at Kilimanjaro International Airport and was met by the Pastor and his family with whom I had previously corresponded with, was driven to the nearest town called Moshi, and was booked into the Y.M.C.A. During that first week in Africa, I was heavily burdened by all that had happened in the country of Tanzania and the Continent of Africa. From the colonists taking precious resources to the 'slave trade,' I began to feel the pain of the country and of all the abuses that had been perpetrated against the people. Julius Kambarage Nyrere, who the local people called the "Father of the Nation" (1922-1999), had just died, and it was a month of mourning for the people. I went to the ruling party headquarters and signed the condolence book.

I was having great difficulty eating and sleeping. It was like an enforced fast, and I didn't quite know what to make of it all. For two nights I kept receiving the same two words, "Pilgrim Progress", "Pilgrim Progress" I would turn over on my left side and try to sleep, "Pilgrim

Progress." Then I turn over on my right side, "Pilgrim Progress." What on earth was going on with this "Pilgrim Progress?" At 6:00 a.m. in the morning, I had had enough. I had cried for Tanzania, I had fasted, and now I couldn't sleep, so it was time to take action. "Lord, this is what I am going to do. I am going downstairs and I am going to eat a good hearty breakfast. I will then go to the front of this building, stand on the steps and say, "Holy Spirit, 'guide me, lead me, teach me, and show me as to why I am here in Moshi, Tanzania, East Africa."

So I did just that. I started walking through the gates of the Y.M.C.A, and my first observation was that there were no footpaths, and the drivers trying to negotiate the round-a-bout appeared to have a 'death wish' as the drivers juggled for positions instead of driving in an orderly manner. I persevered until I had crossed the road and was now walking on what appeared to be a sort of path going towards the town center. I met my first leper begging on the street. As she held out her hand to receive some money, I could see that her finger digits were all missing and her hand was just a stump. A women in a colourful piece of material was carrying a large piece of wood on her head and a baby attached to her back by a piece of material that was wrapped around her and the baby. As I took all these different sights in, I was aware that everything was just 'so different'. I walked down the road until I came to a T junction. I didn't know whether I should cross the road or not and just stood there. I turned around and saw a Catholic bookshop and sensed that I should go into the shop. I was a little hesitant about this request not being a catholic myself, and decided I would just take a look at the window display. I still sensed that I should go inside the bookshop, so I plucked up courage and walked through the front door. "Karibu" "welcome", I was warmly greeted by the staff and I started to wander around the shop and look at the many Christian artifacts that were for sale. On a table, I saw a large pile of 'old' A4 size second hand publications and casually started to look through the pile. "Wow!" Lo and behold there was an old copy of 'Pilgrim Progress.' I snatched the book from the pile and opened it up.

My heart took an extra beat of sheer joy when I saw that this book was in picture form with English sub-titles. I looked up to heaven and spoke out loud, "God thank you. You know that I am such a simple person and that I had great difficulty reading Pilgrim Progress by John Bunyan as a teenager with all the thees, the theys, and the thou's that I never got passed the fourth chapter, but now it is all in picture form in English, so there just has to be something in this book for me." I paid the nun behind the desk who had quizzically been watching me as I spoke to the heavens, and I hurried back down the road to the Y.M.C.A.

I sat on my bed as I started to pour over the pictures and the text. It was the story of a man called Christian, who had a large burden on his back, and he knows that the only way he can lose his burden is to follow 'the way' to Jesus Christ. When I came to the picture of Christian waving 'goodbye' to his wife and family, I felt a painful stab in my heart, as I realized that God might be asking me to do the same thing; leave my family and follow 'the way'.

I went downstairs to the dining room and had some lunch. I then walked to the front door and once again spoke the words that I had said in the morning which had led me to the bookshop.

"Holy Spirit, guide me, lead me, teach me, show me as to why I am here in Tanzania."

I started walking in the hot mid-day sun. I passed the catholic bookshop where I had found the paperback book and now continued down the road. I passed the police station and carried on walking. I came to a Hindu temple on the corner, and I took a left turn and crossed the road. Half way down the street I stopped. I couldn't sense the presence of the Holy Spirit leading me anymore. "Now what?" I thought and leant my back against a wall. I looked across the road the sign said HIV/AIDS Information Center. Then I sensed that I was supposed to go inside the centre. At this terrifying thought I was definitely going to 'put my foot down.' Absolutely no way would I ever go into a place like that, the only thing that I have in my brain data about this HIV/AIDS virus is that Princess Diana shook hands without wearing a pair of gloves and the Queen of England always did. That's it, sum total of brain data.

I felt a warm sense on the back of my neck as I found myself walking across the road towards the center door. Once again on this journey, I was finding myself in a place of confusion and discomfort as I opened the door of the HIV/AIDS Information Center and walked inside. I turned around after closing the door behind me and stood there absolutely mortified! There were platform seats on either side of a walkway and on these platforms were people whose bodies were so wasted and thin, and their eyes were sunken in their sockets as they all turned from the television screen that they were watching to stare at me. "Oh dear God, save me from this situation," I prayed. "Can I catch AIDS by standing here? Is it an airborne disease? Oh dear God, what have You gotten me in to now?" I was sending up arrow prayers one after the other in quick succession, I was both scared and afraid of the situation that I found myself in. I saw a man standing in one corner wearing a white coat, and I hesitantly started to walk towards him aware of all those sunken eyes watching my every move. As I approached the man, I considered what I was going to say. "Excuse me sir, do you have any brochures or pamphlets about the HIV/AIDS virus please?" With just a smile on his face and without answering, he opened the door that he was standing near and ushered me into a room full of very busy African ladies. I was welcomed to come and sit down on a sofa and was asked if I would like a cup of tea or a soda. Thinking it through, I decided that it was probably safer to drink from a bottle than a cup, just in case it hadn't been washed properly and there were HIV/AIDS germs on the cup (how terribly ignorant I was at this time). I explained to this lady, who spoke very good English, that I was just enquiring about the effects that the virus was having on the community. Seeing my interest, the lady asked me if I would like to join a group of ladies which were going on a safari the following Saturday to a place called Same to distribute school uniforms to the many orphans, and I agreed to the suggestions.

A Land Rover arrived with a group of ladies inside, and we started the journey which was to take over an hour. A road had been cut out of part of the Usumbara mountain by the villagers, and it looked extremely dangerous as only one vehicle could access the steep mountain road at any one time. Cows and goats were negotiating a small ledge of the road as we started the steep climb, and once again, my arrow prayers were being posted to heaven in an effort to stop the Land Rover from going over the edge and crashing down the mountainside. When we thankfully arrived at our destination, a large group of people were awaiting our arrival. With song and dance and branch waving, we were ushered over to a field where many children were sat just waiting for the gifts to be distributed. I was surprised at how many of the children looked so malnourished and sick. Was this due to the illness or because there was no food for the children to eat? I didn't know. After the distribution, we descended the mountain road, and I only felt safe when all four wheels of the Land Rover were safely placed back on to the tarmac road once again. The ladies asked me if I would like to accompany them the following week to distribute more school uniforms to more orphans on the foothills of Mount Kilimanjaro, to which I readily agreed.

As the vehicle climbed up to 6,000 feet, I decided to try to relax and enjoy the countryside with its many coffee and banana plantations. I pondered if the Garden of Eden had been as verdant as this area appeared to be. On our arrival at an uncompleted church with a field, we once again saw lots of sick looking children staring at us and my heart went out to them. I had overheard a conversation about a little five year old girl who was covered in boils and living on the streets, and no one would touch her because she had AIDS. This was my first introduction to stigmatization. This story was to plague my mind and it wrenched my heart that a young child could die all alone and in pain and not have anyone to help or to love her or to show her the love of Jesus.

We had, in our group of ladies, a local social worker, and I asked her a question of which the answer was going to change my life. "What is going to happen to all these children? There are just so many of them. And they all look so sick." She replied, "A percentage of the children that you see here today will die of malnutrition as there is no one who will feed them. Another percentage will die of the opportunist infections as their parents have already succumbed to the virus. Another percentage will die of treatable diseases like malaria, but because there is no one who will purchase the drugs for them, they too will die, so only a small percentage that you see here today will actually survive to adulthood."

(There were no anti-retro viral drugs available in the country at this time.)

I returned to the UK, and it was now Christmas time. My family all concluded that I had gotten over the African experience and everything would now return back to normal. How completely wrong they were.

We welcomed in the 21st century and the predicted catastrophes from the computers going berserk didn't happen but something of biblical proportions did.

I was busy doing something menial in the kitchen when all of a sudden I had a 'mind's eye picture again, or some would perhaps say a vision, and just like the 'fruit cake' picture this one was also in three parts.

From the first position, I could see Jesus standing in front of me, and he was so 'huge'. He was wearing a long white gown, his arms were held out and long cowl sleeves draped over his arms. From the second position, I could see myself as a small child looking up into the face of Jesus, and in my arms I was holding a dead child. And Jesus spoke these words to me: "Deliver these children safely into my arms". The picture then disappeared, and I was then consumed with this exquisite feeling of pure love that ran from my head to my toes and back again. The feeling was totally indescribable. Liquid love flowed through my veins and totally consumed me. I didn't want to move out of the moment and just stood there, praising and singing to my Lord.

After this happened to me, I wanted to be left alone in total solitude and not to be disturbed by everyday normal things. I could understand for the very first time why monks lived in monasteries and hermits lived in caves. I just felt that I didn't want to be contaminated by the outside world with all of its wars and people doing bad and cruel things to each other; what I had tasted, I didn't want to tarnish. I just wanted my life to encompass pure love.

Of course, this kind of behavior was not acceptable to everyone else, least of all my family.

I can look back now and see that this action was my preparation time for me to prepare myself for going to live in Africa, but my family thought that I had "totally lost it" altogether. The time that I spent meditating and praying made me more determined that I was going to go back to help those Tanzanian children who were suffering so much with no one to help or care for them in their terminal illness. "If I only helped one or two children," I thought, "it would be worth the sacrifice."

I asked my husband to join me on this quest, but he already had his own opinion of my 'outlandish' behavior, and as a non-Christian, I could see he 'didn't get it either'.

With this decision firmly made in my mind to move to Tanzania, I sold or gave away everything that I owned, and I was going to practically do what Jesus said in the bible, "Sell everything that you own and follow me" (Mark 10 v 21).

CHAPTER FIVE
THE MOVE

It was June 1st 2000, my family and friends gathered at a restaurant to wish me 'Bon Voyage'. The following day, I boarded a small aircraft at Humberside Airport and landed in Amsterdam. After a couple of hours lay-over, I then boarded a KLM flight to Kilimanjaro International Airport where a car was waiting to take me once again the 40 kilometers to the Y.M.C.A. in Moshi - the venue that I had stayed at six months earlier.

Pastor Patrick (not his real name) was eager to introduce me to his family and friends, and I was kindly invited into the home of a resident Professor and her husband who worked at the main training hospital. As they were going on tour of the USA, they asked if I would like to occupy their lovely home whilst they were away, but before they left they had one more job to do and that was to preach a sermon at a newly opened bible school up on the foothills of Mount Kilimanjaro. I was also asked if I would like to speak on the 'gifts of the 'Holy Spirit'.

We arrived at a large compound with a security wall around the perimeter and were invited to be seated on wooden platforms.

The Pastor of the bible school, whom I shall call Pastor Malcolm, made the opening introductions.

After the Professor had given her sermon (thankfully in English, which was then transposed into the Kiswahili language), we took a break for a cup of tea and bites.

Whilst sat at the table, I glanced around the room and noticed in a store room there were some baby cribs. We finished our light refreshments and went back into the room and now it was my turn to speak. After I sat back down again, I sensed a question forming in my mind. "Aren't you curious as to why a bible school has baby cribs?" "Oh yes" I wondered why, and my thoughts moved on. Once again, the question was posed to me, "Aren't you curious as to why there are baby cribs at a bible school?"

The grace was said to bring the meeting to a close, and the group moved off towards the vehicle. I turned and asked Pastor Malcolm the question that had visited my mind on two occasions. "Why do you have baby cots in your store room?", I asked. "That's because three years ago these buildings used to be an orphanage", he replied. My curiosity satisfied, I climbed in to the vehicle, and we left to return down the steep mountain to Moshi.

Everything was just so 'different' to what I had been used to, and I could see quite a lot of adjustment and understanding was going to be required on my part.

After living in the bungalow on the hospital campus for two weeks, the building of the bible school repeatedly came into my mind. I laid down a fleece: "Lord, if you want me to make contact about this building, You have to arrange a meeting for me to meet with the Pastor from the bible school."

A week later, Pastor Patrick visited me with his wife, and during the conversation, he mentioned Pastor Malcolm. "Do you think you could ask Pastor Malcolm to call and see me? I have something I would like to discuss with him," I asked. Seven days later Pastor Malcolm arrived at the house. By the end of the visit, we had made a verbal agreement for me to open a children's home at his facility, and I would help him to establish a bible school – after all we were both serving the same God, so why would we need a legal document to be written? And that was my first very Big mistake.

The agreement was that I would renovate the buildings and use them as a children's home whilst Pastor Malcolm obtained all the necessary operating licenses that were required by the local social welfare department. I would in turn provide financial support to his bible school and students, and through both these services, we would be able to give "God the Glory".

Three days prior to the Professor and her husband returning home, I had made arrangements for a vehicle to come and take me and my four plastic bags, a word processor plus a dog up the mountain to the center.

A local doctor, having heard of my plans to live on the mountain with the 'Chagga' tribe, allowed me to choose an eighteen month old black South African ridgeback whom I named "Sasha." She quickly became my loyal friend.

CHAPTER SIX

PANYA BUKA

A s I checked the bungalow to make sure that I had not left anything behind, I heard the vehicle arriving, its tyres crunching on the gravel outside, then squealing to a halt. I walked out into a light September rain to greet the Pastor who had agreed to be my 'removal' man and take me to my new home on Mount Kilimanjaro.

As I placed my belongings into the back of the covered pick-up truck and waited for the reluctant dog to be physically man-handled in to the back, I noticed the canvas showing on the back of the rear tyre. "Oh my goodness!" Is it safe to get in to this vehicle?" I thought. Having newly arrived in the country, I could still recall the stringent UK driving rules and allowing bald tyres on a vehicle was definitely not one of them. How could this obviously un-roadworthy vehicle be allowed on the road? This first observation was my first challenge that 'things worked in a developing country somewhat differently to my countries rules and regulations'.

Hesitantly, I sat in the front seat next to the Pastor and automatically turned to put on my seat belt. There wasn't one. For the umpteenth time, I wondered if I was doing the right thing and considered getting out of the vehicle. The truck was now reversing out of the driveway. I sat placidly in the seat praying, only answering a question when the pastor wanted to converse with me.

We left Moshi and drove along the Arusha road, and we turned right at Kwasadala market and started the steep climb up the mountain. As we crawled forward, it was difficult to see out of the front window as my windshield wiper didn't work, but thankfully the driver's did. As I sat there I had time to contemplate my actions. All the critical comments came flooding into my mind of "how crazy my actions were" – how could God possibly use such an unworthy vessel as myself? But this deep seated inner conviction that I felt that I was doing the right thing gave me the courage to continue on this extraordinary journey.

Jolted back from my thoughts, I realized my arm was feeling wet and cold from the window that didn't close, and I started to feel despondent.

The mud mountain road appeared to be slippery as I heard the Pastor change the manual gears from second to first. Looking out of the side window, I was suddenly aware of excited children's voices shouting and screaming. I moved closer to the window to try to see what the noise was all about. One child in a group of children was holding something in his hand and swinging it around his head. As we drew closer, I could see it was the biggest rat that I had ever seen, and I let out a 'shriek' of horror. Its very long tail that the child was holding and swinging around must have been easily 12" long and its body another 6". Startled by my outburst, the driver looked away from his concentrated effort of driving and keeping the truck on the road and said; "That's a maize rat, it's a panya buka," and he went back to his driving. They have rats here on the mountain as big as well fed cats! Whilst making preparations for my trip to Africa, I had watched the channels on the television that showed the national parks of Tanzania. I was aware of the yearly migration of the Wildebeest and knew the local Arusha National Wild life park was just 50 minutes away from where I would be living but this was something else.

I settled back in my seat, trying to digest the 'size issue' of the rat, when all engine power to the truck failed. The car stalled and stopped.

A look of grave concern came over the Pastor's face as he applied the brakes to try to stop the vehicle rolling backwards down the mountain, but all that did was to make the truck start to slide to the left of the road where the valley was. Stunned and realizing what was happening, I opened the truck door and jumped out of the moving truck. I was slipping and sliding on the mud and trying to hold the truck whilst I looked around for some rocks to put under the wheels to try to stop the backward movement of the vehicle. But it was all too late; gravity was having its way, and the vehicle continued moving crab-like across the road to the approaching disaster which was about to happen as the truck would go over the edge of the road and crash down to the valley below.

I watched helplessly as the inevitable was going to happen. I remembered snatches of Psalm 91 v 2 (Good News Bible) that I had prayed before I had left the bungalow that morning, the prayer of protection: "You are my defender and protector, You are my God in whom I trust; (3) He will keep you safe from all hidden dangers and from all deadly diseases. (4) He will cover you with his wings; you will be safe in his care; his faithfulness will protect and defend you. (5) You need not fear any dangers at night or sudden attacks during the day or the plague that strikes in the dark or the evils that kill in the daylight."

Verse 15 of this same Psalm says, " When they call to me, I will answer them." "God, I'm calling on your help, right now!"

I watched as the rear wheels of the truck went over the edge of the road, and I screamed out loud. Time stood still. Then it was all over.

The truck had hit a group of banana tree's which was screeching under the weight of the rear wheels. I started to climb down the steep bank holding onto the truck for support. I had to get the dog and my bags out of the truck before it crashed to the valley below.

I could see people running up the road towards us, and as I surveyed the scene of two wheels straddling over the edge and stuck in banana trees, I waited for the tree's to collapse under the weight and for the vehicle to plunge into the valley below and perhaps burst into flames.

The Pastor was now directing men to help in this strange dialectic tongue of the Chagga language as I stood in the middle of the road, the drizzling rain wetting my hair and sticking it to my forehead as I held the 'muddy' rope with the dog attached at the other end. And I knew I had a decision to make. Did I start to walk down the mountain back to Moshi and arrange to fly back to the UK? I still had the money from the sale of all my 'goods and chattels' so I could easily start all over again, or, do I continue this journey, on which I believed God had sent me to fulfill to love the un-lovable who were stigmatized and abused and who had no-one to show them the love of Jesus in their lives. I started to walk up the muddy steep mountain road to my new home.

CHAPTER SEVEN
IMPOSTER OF A PASTOR

I purchased lots of different colored paints as I wanted the children's home to be as bright and colorful as possible. I employed a carpenter to build a new fitted kitchen and six double decker beds. The baby cribs which I had previously seen in the store were pulled out and re-painted and placed in the nursery. There was no water on tap, and I had to employ a lady to fetch and carry buckets of water on her head from the local spring down the side of the mountain. This was a journey that took two hours each day.

The electricity bill had not been paid and the power had been cut off, so I had no water and no electricity until I deemed to pay the Pastors large back unpaid bill. I was busy painting a wall in a room which would eventually become the dormitory when I heard the drums start to beat. "What does it mean?" I wondered. My mind thought of all the African movies that I had watched where the drum beats out a message to other villages to pass on information. Were the drums informing people that a white women was now living on their mountain? And what would the consequences be? Before my mind went too far with all the possibilities, I decided to speak to the security guard whom I had employed who spoke relatively good English. I peeled off the latex gloves which were covered in paint and went to find the man. The drums, he explained, was the butcher informing the villagers that a cow had been slaughtered and meat was now ready for sale. Thank goodness for that I thought! The guard pointed to the 10' high security gate and told me there were people outside the gate wanting to see me. "What for?" I replied "Why do these people want to see me?" "Mama," he replied, "you have to understand that it is not only orphans who are dying of hunger but the elderly too. If they have no one to care for them, they are expected to lay down and die! I can take you to such an old man right now who is lying on the mud floor just waiting to die."

Appalled to hear such news, I told the guard that I needed to see for myself and please ask the people to return in three days' time when I had arranged for an interpreter to be present and then I would see how I could help them.

I purchased a 50 kilo sack of rice and separated it into 1 kilo bags. Then hiring porters to carry the rice/meat/vegetables that I had purchased, I climbed the mountain to the village where the old man lived. I was taken to meet him, and indeed he was lying outside on the mud floor. He was so weak, he could hardly raise his hand to take hold of mine. The porters gently lifted him up to a sitting position. He was so thin and weak you could see his rib cage, and I quickly paid for someone to cook the food for the old man each day until I would return the following Friday. He took my hand and turned it over and said to the porters, "Look, this Mzungu (European) has five fingers just like me!" How many fingers he thought a white women should have I wasn't quite sure but my happiest moment was six weeks later, when the old man heard children running to catch up with our party as I always carried sweets with me to give them. I was aware that this was probably the first time some of these children had met a white women and knew I would have to earn their trust. The old man, leaning heavily on his stick, slowly walked up the path to greet us. Now that was sheer joy to see that I could make a difference to someone's life, and he in turn was overjoyed at the new mattress and sheets we had brought for him to lie upon.

I established a pattern, and carrying a back pack with lots of water for drinking, I would make the same trip climbing higher up the foothills to take food to the hungry. This was the first food program that I started.

I was then asked by the local people if I would help pay for medicines for the poor who had no money to obtain medical treatment, so I made an arrangement with a local dispensary that if they received a letter from me with my signature, I would pay the medical bills of the children and adults at the end of the month. Thankfully many lives were saved, especially young children who suffered from malaria; their families couldn't afford the anti-malaria drugs which cost around 40 pence.

Before one child had come into care, I now had two programs running, and I was given a new name: The stick of Jesus.

When this old blind lady who we were visiting made the porters laugh as I handed her some food one day, I asked them what they were laughing at. They replied that the old lady had called me the 'Stick of Jesus,' and when they asked her 'why do you call mama that name?' she had replied that, when you get old, you need a stick to support yourself and that was what the mama was doing. Jesus had sent her to the mountain to be her stick!

Not long after these programs had started, other Pastors from different villages were visiting with me to tell me that they too had hungry children in their villages, and would I please offer assistance to them.

I replied, "you find me five cases who you consider need the most help and I will visit with them."

As the group of porters, Pastor Alfred - a Pastor from one of the villages requesting help - and myself walked along the dirt paths past the banana groves and straddling the water channels which irrigated the crops, we came to the first home that the Pastor had identified. He told me an elderly lady lived in this mud stick hut which had been covered with cow dung. He shouted the familiar words as we approached the hut to let the householder know visitors were approaching. "Hodi, hodi," and from inside the hut the familiar "karibu, karibu," welcome was clearly heard. The hut was only large enough to take the Pastor and myself so the porters had to sit and wait on the grass outside. When my eye's adjusted to the darkness I could see there was nothing inside the single room hut except some old banana leaves in the corner with a few bits of material on top of them, obviously this was the bed of the elderly lady. The Pastor moved over to the corner and lifted up a banana leaf and whispered something to the lady before coming over to speak to me. "As you can see she owns nothing and has no food. Even the banana leaves are full of insects, and I have asked her to change them and put some clean ones down," he said. At this comment I left the hut, went outside and sat on the grass with the porters, and opened up my back pack and took out my notebook. Item (1) Make a small single bed and provide a mattress, sheets and blankets and a weekly food supply. I went back inside and asked the lady if the Pastor and I could pray for her. I told her of my plans to help her, and asked would she like my help. The old lady started to weep, and we left her holding on very tightly to the rice, meat, and vegetables that we had given her to last for a whole week. I could see I would have to make a Wednesday of the week for a food program in this locality if I was to see other people so desperate as this old lady.

The next home we called at was for a young boy who was experiencing constant nose bleeds. The family had been told we were coming and the young boy was sitting on the porch awaiting our arrival. He had a piece of dirty blooded material which was tied underneath his nose.

After the usual greetings, a chair was brought out for me to sit upon. I placed a pair of disposable gloves on my hands and started to remove the cloth bandage. I was informed by the mother that the child would just start with heavy nose bleeds, which had been going on for years, and made him so weak that he would just lie down for long periods in a weakened state, and his family could not afford for the operation that they were told the boy needed to stop the nose bleeds. I took some clean bandages out of my first aid kit and gave them to the boy's mother and with another one, proceeded to wrap it under the boys nose, as a trickle of blood was still oozing away. I asked the boy's parents to take the boy to the dispensary that I was working with to obtain a referral letter to the main hospital in Moshi, and when an appointment was made, I would supply the funds to open a file and for the boy to have the necessary operation. The group laid hands on the child and prayed for him. After saying our 'goodbyes', we moved on to our next call. Pastor Alfred informed the group that an elderly lady had been left with two grandchildren after their mother had ran away and the father was out looking for work. They had no food to eat in the mud/stick hut when he had called the day before to say we would visit today. I spotted a very thin old lady walking very slowly towards me. As I went forward to give her a hug, she literally collapsed into my arms, and we both fell backwards. Willing hands from the porters rushed to help the lady up from on top of me, and she started to silently weep. Brushing myself down, I spotted two little children staring at me from behind the mud hut. I asked the Pastor to minister to the elderly lady whilst I went over to the children. On my approach they both ran off. I went over to the hut and there wasn't even a door hanging on it. "But, what about the animals entering the hut at night," I thought. "The scorpions, the snakes, and definitely the rats. How can they live like this, and no neighbor willing to help the poor old lady, and her son not even replacing the broken door on the hut to protect his children." I cannot understand what poverty does to the mind. Hopelessness, I came to learn, slowly eats away at the soul, until doing nothing is better than doing something. When I looked inside the darkened hut, all that was inside were some ashes on the floor where a fire had once been lit and a piece of sack cloth on the floor where the grandmother and the children slept. I returned to the group and asked one of the porters if he would give the children some sweets, and if possible without frightening or dragging them, to bring them over so that I could take a closer look at them. I sat on the ground next to the old lady and opened up my lunch box for her to eat my remaining bread. When the children saw their grandmother eating food, they came and sat by her side. I could see the older child, who looked to be around three years of age, looked sick, as her brown eyes didn't quite look right, and I asked Pastor Alfred for his opinion. "I think she might have malaria and something else, and by looking at their stomachs I would suggest that both children are full of worms." "Ask the lady if she has given the children any food today please," I prompted. She replied that she had no flour to make any porridge with. (you mix flour and water together and this is what the poor eat for breakfast and call it porridge, and for an evening meal they add more flour to the water to make a stiff consistency like a dough, and this is called ugali) A diet of this leads to Kwasha Koo, or Marasmas, which is a protein deficiency which children can die from. "All the 'bibi' (grandmother) has given them are two mashed up green banana's", replied the Pastor.

The porters found some wood to start a fire, and when the rice and meat was cooking, we left the old women and the children saying we would be back the following day to take the children to a dispensary and arrange with the social welfare department to bring the children into care. These two little girls of 3 years and eighteen months were the first two children to come to live with me at the center.

Pastor Malcolm by now had managed to obtain the licenses to operate the children's home, and after the girls arrived, they were quickly followed by an abandoned baby boy whom twelve police officers escorted to our center. "God's children were starting to arrive."

A Chairman of a village way up the mountain in an area that I had not visited before sent a 'runner' to me with a letter requesting for help with three vulnerable children whose parents had already died.

I made provisions for the climb and employed porters for the day to accompany me along with Pastor Alfred who was going to be my interpreter. Three times en-route to the village, I had to stop and rest due to the intense heat and the steepness of the climb.

When we eventually arrived at the dwelling, I just collapsed on some grass. My blouse was absolutely soaked and stuck to my skin with perspiration, and I quickly downed a liter of water. As I drained the last drops from the plastic bottle of Kilimanjaro water, I spotted a young girl slowly walking up the hill. She was painfully thin and about eight years of age, and I could see she was carrying a bundle in her kanga (material) on her back. A porter offered me a hand and helped to pull me to my feet as the young girl approached me. Without looking into my face, she did a little curtsey. I moved to look at the child she was carrying, and I could see a baby with a very thin hollow face and large staring eyes look back at me. I thought the baby was perhaps around three months of age. The girl, who had a plastic mug in her hand, had just visited a neighbor's house to try to obtain milk for her baby brother. We were informed that the girl's younger brother had been scalded on his head and had been taken to hospital. The Chairperson was right; these children definitely needed some nurturing, so our new family grew by three more.

I had lived on the mountain now for four months, and everything was going great. The brand new fitted kitchen looked smart and clean. I had worked really hard painting all the walls and cement floors. The new double decker beds were neatly in rows in the dormitory. Then Pastor Malcolm dropped the first of his many bombshells. He demanded that I pay him an outrageous sum of money for rent each week, the equivalent to the rent of a mansion house in Moshi.

I was flabbergasted at this new turn of events and it threw me into total confusion. "But we had an agreement," I said lamely. "We agreed that I would renovate and modernize your property, and you would obtain the operating licenses. When you had some theology students, I would help to support them with food and expenses. We both agreed in the Professor's bungalow that we would both be serving a 'higher purpose' than our own. What's changed?" The man became most insistent and demanded that I pay him weekly rent money even though I had spent over 6,000.00 pound sterling making renovations on his property. "OK" I said, "It looks to me as if you have deliberately waited until I had children living here and spent all this money on your property. You're now making this outlandish demand for rent when there is not even any water on the premises, and I have had to pay your unpaid electricity bills just so that we have electricity on the premises, and that is so spasmodic, we are lucky if we have ten days supply a month!" The man stood in front of me and still demanded I pay him rent money.

"Well, I'm going to pay you what you are asking for in rent, and then I'm going to pray about this situation," I said, and I did.

Just before my first African Christmas, I was brought a new-born baby who had the HIV/AIDS virus and his mother had died in childbirth. It was whilst I was feeding him his late-night bottle and reading scriptures that I received the answer to my prayers. And the word came, "IMPOSTER OF A PASTOR. IMPOSTER OF A PASTOR." The next time that I saw the pastor, as he didn't live locally, I told him that I had heard the word from God and the word was that he was an IMPOSTER OF A PASTOR. (I was later to find out that he neither had a church nor a flock) I also wanted to know why he wanted the money from me. He replied that he was going to receive twenty three students on the sixth January and he needed the money to prepare for them. "Just in case that I have the message completely wrong I am going to pay you the rent money up to the January 6th and if twenty three students arrive, I will know that I am wrong, but if they do not arrive, I will know the message that I have received is correct, and I will stop the payments." When the 6th of January arrived, only he and his nephew came to the center.

I agonized an awful lot over this situation, and I realized that I had honestly believed that a man who called himself a "minister of the cloth" had to be an Honorable man, as all the Pastors whom I had met over the years had all been Honorable men and women so I brought these precepts of honesty, justice, accountability, and the love of God that I knew that they had in their life, over with me from the UK. I was shocked, perhaps a little naive, and totally unprepared for a culture of people who would use the word of God to say anything to a European if it meant that they could extract finances from them.

God was now in control of my life and I had lessons to be learnt. He was about to turn up the refining fire in my life. Big Time.

CHAPTER EIGHT

A LAMB IN THE WOLVES LAIR

I am sending you out as sheep amongst wolves. (Mathew 10 : 16) Jesus sent His disciples out to preach to the lost sheep of Israel, and he gave the disciples instructions as to what to do and what to say, and when they were being persecuted, to allow the Holy Spirit to speak on their behalf. I found myself in a similar position as I was a lamb sleeping in the lair of a wolf, and even trying to encourage dialogue and a practical solution to the problem of the 'rent issue' appeared to be a useless proposition. He did not care about the children's welfare; all he wanted was the 'money'. I would have been prepared to pay him a smaller amount of rent, but not the huge amount that he was demanding.

I received a hand delivered letter from the local Immigration department requesting that I attend for an interview. When I attended with Pastor Alfred, I learnt that a 'damning' letter had been received by them accusing me of – wait for it – beating the staff and holding orgies! Of course, I fiercely denied these absurd allegations, and I was also informed that the letter suggested that I should be deported.

More interviews followed along with more scandalous letters. I thought it was time to engage a lawyer to represent me, and I gave him a letter that I had just received written in Kiswahili. It was so bad that the lawyer refused to interpret the letter! It suggested all manner of bad things that I was supposed to be doing and being accused of. "How can all this possibly be happening to me," I thought "when all that I am trying to do is to help the children and the community."

But this was nothing compared to what was going to happen. The heat was now going to be turned up to 'full blast'.

At the same time as all this was happening probably due to the negotiation of the Pastor, I was also told to close the centre down and disburse the children. I was frantic with worry. No reason was given, and nothing was placed in writing.

Over a ten year period of living in Tanzania, I have constantly had a 'thorn in my flesh" (2 Corinthians chapter 12 : 7), and on five occasions I was told to close the homes down, due to my refusal to "pay the brown envelope." The police were even brought into the compound to enforce closure which of course absolutely terrified the children who thought 'their' mama was going to be taken to prison.

But you see, if I was standing for Jesus Christ, I couldn't pay the unofficial money, and so what I have done on every occasion is to lock myself into my room for five days, fasting and praying. During this time with God, I pour out my soul and the problems to my Lord, and on the last day, I give everything over to Him. "Lord, if you want these 'precious' children, who are fatherless and motherless, to return to the streets and be stigmatized and have no future except of being abused, and if you want me to return to the UK, then so be it, but knowing the love that you have for these children, I don't believe you will allow this to happen. I am now going to stand back and watch you move mountains to protect these children." And He has. On five occasions, he brought forth a strong, believing, Christian Tanzanian man with a servant's heart to stop the closures.

My 'thorn' was eventually pulled out of my side after ten years of sheer misery and despair. (Matthew 10 : 26 Living Bible) "But don't be afraid of those who threaten you. For the time is coming when the truth will be revealed: their secret plots will become public information."

I can hear my mother's words of wisdom which she would always repeat, and they were: "God doesn't pay his debts with money." At these very stressful times, I was often asked, "But why do you stay and put up with all of this abuse?" The only answer I could give was that, when that first abandoned baby came into my arms, my heart was purchased to love and care for him and all of the other children who had no one to call their own, and I love them all. It is my privilege to serve them and to ensure that they have a good education and an opportunity to become the person that God wants them to be. If one child dies unnecessarily, Tanzania loses the next generation from that child, and with the pandemic caused by the AIDS virus, which decimated the population, I felt I had to stay and try to help the country by providing the next generation with the tools necessary to become 'good' Tanzanian citizens instead of some of them ending up in the prison system and their lives being one of misery and unhappiness.

In these early days of my life being lived in Tanzania and these two 'whammies' hitting me simultaneously, I made a decision and that was: Tanzania could have my time, because that's mine to give away. Tanzania can even have my life, because that's mine to give away too, but what Tanzania will never have is my integrity, for I will take that to the grave with me.

CHAPTER NINE
POWERS OF PRINCIPALITIES AND DARKNESS

I t was another beautiful Friday on the foothills of Mount Kilimanjaro as the porters gathered at the children's home and enjoyed a hot cup of spiced tea before we started out on what would be a long day's trek delivering food to the poor on the mountain slopes. The 50 kilo sack of rice that I purchased each week had now been divided into one kilo bags and was distributed throughout the porters back packs along with kilo's of meat we had acquired from our neighbor, the butcher. We started our climb light heartedly, and people were now coming out of their homes to come and shake our hands and thank me for helping their neighbors. The children would tag along with our party as they knew each week they saw me, there would be some sweets for them. It was a merry band of travelers as we slogged up the steep mountain paths. We were passing a house which was set back off the mud path, when a women came rushing down the driveway shouting "mzungu subiri" "mzungu subiri", which means "wait European." The party stopped and waited for her to explain to the Pastor who was with us what and she wanted. Pastor Alfred, who was my interpreter for that day, said that the women wanted the wazungu to go and pray for her daughter whose hand was badly infected. The party walked up to the little house and around the back where the women went indoors and brought out two chairs for the Pastor and myself to sit upon. After we were seated, a young girl of around seventeen years of age was brought out from inside the house with her hand wrapped in a dirty piece of material. I asked Pastor Alfred to find out what the problem was whilst I put on a pair of examination gloves. The lady of the house said her daughter had not been out of the house for over two years as she had a terrible fear of going outside. At the same time as this fear of the outside came, her hand started to become inflamed. It started with just one finger which, overtime, had spread to another and then another. This infection had now spread right up her left arm. The lady thought, in her opinion, a witchdoctor had placed a curse on her daughter. "Yes, sure," I thought sarcastically. After removing the last piece of material, the horribly infected hand and arm was exposed. Each finger was badly swollen and puffed up and running puss. I went over to the rucksack where the porter had placed it on the ground next to where he sat, and rummaged for our First Aid Kit which held the necessary bandages and cleaning solution that I would need. Pastor Alfred said he would pray for the girl as I prepared to clean all the dirt and debris from the girls arm. He went behind the girls chair and placed his hands on her shoulder and started praying as the girl sat and allowed me to attend to her wounds. This would only be a stop-gap measure until I could take the girl to a local dispensary for some antibiotics and pay the bill. As I started to bandage at the top of her arm, she started to flay her arm around, and I was having difficulty following her movements. The Pastor started praying louder, and the more he prayed the more the girl twisted and turned on the chair. It was now quite impossible for me to continue, and the roll of bandage flew out of my hand. The porters came over to hold the girl, but she then started kicking and squealing, and I moved further away. The girl then started to speak in a low, squeaky, eerie man's voice. The Pastor raised his voice louder. The girl was now struggling more and speaking in this low man's voice. "What's going on," I asked the Pastor. "Why is she behaving like this?" "The girl's full of demons," he said. At this,

I moved away and went and sat on the grass. I reached for my back pack which just happened to contain my bible. I turned to Psalm 91 and started reading it from start to finish, and then started all over again. Holy Bible, Easy to Read version: (1) You can go to God Most-High to hide. You can go to the God All-Powerful for protection. (2) I say to the Lord, You are my place of safety, my fortress, My God I trust you. (3) God will save you from hidden dangers and dangerous diseases. (4) You can go to God for protection, He will protect you like a bird spreading its wings over its babies. God will be like a shield and a wall protecting you. (5) You will have nothing to fear at night. And you won't be afraid of enemy arrows during the day. (6) You will not be afraid of diseases that come in the dark, or terrible sickness that come at noon. (7) You will defeat 1,000 enemies. Your own right hand will defeat 10,000 enemy soldiers. Your enemies will not even touch you! (8) Just look, and you will see that those wicked people are punished! (9) Why? Because you trust the Lord. You made God Most High your place of safety. (10) Nothing bad will happen to you. There will be no diseases in your home. (11) God will command his angels for you, and they will protect you wherever you go. (12) Their hands will catch you, so that you will not hit your foot on a rock. (13) You will have power to walk on lions and poisonous snakes. (14) The Lord says "If a person trusts me. I will save him. I will protect my followers who worship my name." (15) My followers will call to me for help, and I will answer them. I will be with them when they have trouble. I will rescue them and honour them. (16) I will give my followers a long life. And I will save them.

I came to the last verse. I looked up and the girl was still writhing and struggling and screaming in a man's voice. "Oh dear God! What's happening?" I cried out in fear. The Pastor was now demanding the spirits that lived in this girl to leave her at once, and they were screaming and screeching back at him. The girl was totally possessed. I had never witnessed anything like this before, and I was fearful. I started again at the beginning of Psalm 91, this time in a louder voice, because whatever was happening I had to try to protect the Pastor and the porters from this satanic attack. I had read my bible through many times and it always mentioned the enemy, and now the enemy was being very visible in this poor girl. The sacrament came into my mind of how Jesus blood that was shed for me and covers over all my sins. I didn't have any red wine with me but I did have some red coloured juice in my flask. With shaking hands, I poured some into a cup, read Psalm 91 again, and with the bible in one hand and the juice in the other, I went over to the sweating Pastor and the girl being held down by the porters, and said, "In the name of Jesus Christ my Saviour, I pour the blood of the lamb over you," and before I could think what I was doing, I threw the red juice all over the struggling girl and stood back.

The girl looked up at me with eyes full of hate and in a squeaky, eerie, terrifying voice whispered repeatedly in English, "I'm burning. I'm burning. I'm burning." Pastor Alfred responded in English to these demons, "Why are you tormenting this girl? 'What's your name? Come out immediately!" The girls voice responded in perfect English again. "We are many. We will take her arm." At this response, I was totally shocked and freaked out. My mind whirled. This is a peasant girl, and she's speaking in perfect English! How is this remotely possible? "Dear God, protect us from what is happening here." I moved back to the bags and started praying, because this was all beyond me. Ten minutes later, the Pastor came over to me. "I have instructed the demons to go back down. There are far too many in the girl for just me to cast out. I shall have to gather a group of Pastors together to pray for her. You come and pray for her and finish bandaging her arm. She is quiet now, she's exhausted." "Have you done this sort of thing before?" I asked. "How did you know what to do." "Yes," he replied, "we hold a deliverance meeting about every other month. There's a lot of this going on around these parts, lots of old traditions that need binding on earth as it is in heaven."

I really didn't want to go back to where the girl was again. I was fearful as this was right out of my comfort zone. Heavens, I had only been in the country a matter of months, and I was being exposed to situations I had very little understanding about. I knew this sort of exorcism went on in churches, but to have a demon speak in English was totally something I just could not get my head around. The girl was sitting quietly now, and the porters were no longer holding onto her. Her head was drooped on her chest as I gingerly stepped forward once again to try to re-bandage her arm. The porters held her arm out straight, and as I removed the dangling unwound bandage ready to start all over again with a fresh bandage, I started to hum a hymn as I worked. I had completed the arm, and was stood looking at how I was going to place a bandage around the girls fingers, when right in front of my eye's something started to happen. I stared, looking dumb-founded. There in front of my eyes, two fingers on her left hand start-ed to change. Some porters moved back, while others came forward to see what I was mesmerized at. Pastor Alfred came up behind me and stood looking as, right before our very eyes, two fingers became totally healed. I was speechless. The lady of the house, who had in-tently watched everything that happened but preferred to leave Pastor Alfred to deal with this strange phenomenon that was happening with her daughter, started whooping and jumping in the air, the porters started slapping the Pastor on the back, and I just stood there looking in awe and astonishment. "How!? How was this all possible?" The girl had dropped off to sleep with the porter holding her arm up for me. "My God, You are amazing," I thought. I had read many books which boasted of miracles happening and now I was part of one such mira-cle. How? Why? So many questions; my mind was full!

Five days later, a group of five local pastors prayed over the girl and commanded the demons to leave her. The following Friday, we had some volunteers with us from a church that I had attended in Grimsby. They had all heard of the healed two fingers and were anx-iously with their cameras to take film to take back with them to the UK. As we walked the same path again distributing food, the lady of the house was stood waiting, with arms akimbo, for the group to come up the mud path. She hustled all of us around to the back of the house where, once again, she busied herself with finding seats for her honoured guests. When we were all sitting comfortably she went back inside the house and presented the girl.

I stood up to look at her hand as it had no bandage on it. The whole of the hand was completely healed. The guests were able to film the hand and get a report of what happened from the Pastor and myself and film everyone dancing and singing and praising God for the deliverance of this young girl, and it was very strange to receive a copy of the events which were then released and shown on my local TV news channel on their return to the UK.

Each Friday for the following four weeks, we stopped to see the young girl who had now become very friendly and talkative. On the fifth visit we made, her mother told us the girl had gone to visit her sister in Dar es Salaam, a journey by coach of over 500 kilometers. What a changed life from our first visit to this home! A young girl had been healed of her affliction and was now confident enough to travel by herself from her village. What a transformation! This was my first introduction to the powers of demons and principalities which is so clearly mentioned by Jesus in the Bible, as on his three year missionary journey, He caste many demonic forces out of people young and old.

CHAPTER TEN
THE FIRST MIRACLE

When the three children arrived from off the mountain, I took the little baby, whom I had thought to be three months of age, into the nursery to bath, feed and put on some nice clean cloths. I removed the piece of material that was covering him and being used as a nappy/diaper at the same time. I was shocked to find his arms and legs were matchstick thick, and he had a huge extended abdomen. My first thought was this child could not possibly survive.

After I laid him comfortably in one of the cots, he contentedly fell asleep having drunk his formula milk from a bottle. I went into the office to look at the admission file that had been completed with the three children's details. This 'baby' was actually fourteen months of age, but due to the lack of nutrition, he had not reached any of the usual milestones, and had not even attempted to sit up. He just lay on his back, stared, and cried. I considered that this child would be another child that I would 'hand over' into the arms of Jesus.

But God loves to prove me wrong.

Twelve months later, Francis could walk quite majestically, thanks to the amazing effort of our staff, but brother, did he have a bad attitude! I had never met a child quite like Francis before. Whenever he was close to a carer, he would 'lash out' by kicking at them, or just spit at them. We had no idea where he had learnt this behavior from.

We had a volunteer with us at that time who had been very unhappy with her placement in a pre-school through another organization, as she could not cope with young children as young as 5 or 6 years of age being beaten with a stick by the teacher. She had gone into LIA's Dot Internet Café and friends had arranged for the young lady to be brought up the mountain to our center by a passing coffee truck to see if she could complete her placement by helping me with the children.

Jane was such a conscientious worker and just loved working in the nursery with all of the babies. I appreciated her help as I was caring for twelve babies at the time. I had never worked so hard in my life; no sooner had you finished feeding the last baby then the first baby was ready for his bottle. The nursery was like a treadmill of feeding bottles and nappy changes.

Jane would write letters home to her parents telling them all about the children she was helping to care for, and they in turn would pass the letter on to Jane's grandparents who would host 'friendly get-to-gethers' in their home where Jane's letter from Africa would be read out to the group. One gentleman was so touched by the stories that Jane had written about that he asked his friends not to buy him any gifts for his 80th birthday but instead help him to give the children who had the HIV/AIDS virus a 'holiday of a lifetime.' As the anti-retro viral drugs had not arrived in Tanzania at this time, this was certainly a 'death sentence' for the children who carried the virus.

This was a wonderful gift to the children, and everyone had such fun as it was the first time that the children had played on the sand with buckets and spades and collected sea shells and paddled in the Indian Ocean. I returned home with the children with two very badly blistered, sun burnt legs as we had taken a car inner tube with us and I had lain across it in the water and was pushed backwards and forwards by the children for over two hours, a painful lesson learnt.

On our return to the center, Francis started to lose all of his weight gain. It was just dropping off him by the day, and a month later, he looked the same as when I first found him. I took him to the hospital and was told the same thing, "He's terminal. Try to keep him as comfortable and as pain free as you possibly can until he passes over."

Whenever a child was sick or dying, I would not let anyone look after that child but me. I had to make sure I was doing the very best that I could for that sick child, and so a cot was moved into my bedroom so I could nurse Francis. The day came when he fell unconscious, and I sent a 'runner' up the mountain to inform his relatives to come and say their 'goodbyes' to him as I didn't think he would last the night.

As I sat by his cot, I wandered how I should broach the imminent death to his older sister and brother.

The family visited, wailed and cried, and then left. I asked the staff members to all congregate in my bedroom with Francis's sister and brother after they had put the rest of the children to bed that night. We started singing and praising God, as the child lay unconscious. He had a very weak pulse, and I didn't think he would last through the night. Each staff member prayed individually, and then we heard the anguished cries of his brother and sister as they pleaded with God to spare the life of their little brother. We were all in tears and heartbroken. The staff and the two children returned to their rooms, and I continued to keep vigil through the night.

At 5:30 a.m. the next morning, I took a shower and went to find a carer to come and sit with Francis as I had to visit the bank and purchase food supplies. This would take me at least 5-6 hours , but if I left now I could perhaps be back about 11:00 a.m. I gave the carer clear instructions not to disturb him but to just let him 'pass over' peacefully. She sat in my chair beside the cot, and I left to go down the mountain to Moshi.

The back pack was 'bursting at the seams' with supplies as I struggled and sweated back up the steep mountain path. Once again, as I walked, I was having a 'good old moan' to God, as to why He didn't provide me with a vehicle, after all when I was in the UK, I owned two cars, an old Mercedes and a Mitsubishi, so why couldn't I just have one now, it would make my life so much quicker and easier?

But no, I had to accept the fact that this was not going to happen, for my money was dwindling away at a fast rate, and to purchase a car was out of the question. I knocked at the center gate to be allowed in and handed my backpack to the security to take into the kitchen, and then I proceeded along the path to my bedroom. I walked inside and first saw the empty chair. "Where's the carer gone?" I thought. I then moved over to look at Francis in his cot, but he wasn't there. The cot was empty. I stared at the clean white sheet covering the mattress, and at that precise moment in time, I had a picture form in my 'mind's eye'. I could see a rock formation with an opening and a women cautiously bending and looking into a large hole which had been made in the rock. The women stepped back and cried out, "Where have they taken my Lord?" and I said "where have they taken my Francis?" I turned around and slowly walked out of my room on to the path, praying for the soul of Francis as I walked. I turned onto the connecting path to the dining room and looked up, stopped, and stared.

My eyes were seeing but my mind couldn't hold the comprehension. For there was Francis, sitting on a little plastic chair, at a little plastic table, with a plastic spoon in his hand, with a plastic bowl in front of him with food in it, and he was moving his hand in very quick movements getting spoonfuls of food into his mouth as quickly as he could, one mouthful after another.

Word spread like wildfire on the mountain that a miracle had happened in the life of a young child, but what saddened me most about the whole event was that the local people all wanted to know which denomination I belonged to. There was nothing about the fact that Jesus had healed a seriously sick child, but that it must be the church that I attended that had healed the child. From that day on, I have refused to disclose my denomination to the local people and only will say that I stand as a Christian.

When the healing took place, Jesus also did a remake on Franci's personality. Gone was the 'old bad tempered' child, and in its place was a heart for the Lord.

Francis is now fourteen years of age. One day, he was watching his brother play football, and he shouted to him, "Come, and lets go pray together." His brother replied, "No. You go. I'm playing football." Dejectedly, Francis turned away from the pitch and was followed in doors by a carer who heard Francis kneel beside his bed and pray, "God, please forgive my brother for not wanting to pray to you and wanting to play football instead, but I will pray his prayers as well as my own," and he did.

CHAPTER ELEVEN
EMOTIONALLY CHALLENGED

Another referral came in asking for me to accommodate a five year old child whose parents were dying of the HIV/AIDS virus. As it was some distance away, I hired a vehicle to drive to the location, and was accompanied by Pastor Alfred as my interpreter.

We arrived at this impoverished dwelling; the pastor went inside the house whilst I stayed in the vehicle with the driver. Five minutes later, the wooden door opened, and a little boy carrying a blue plastic bag walked out of the house. I opened the car door, and he came straight over to me and climbed into the vehicle. This surprised me, and I thought, "what no tears or hugs or goodbyes?" A frail emaciated women appeared at the door and waved her hand. I waved back, but the boy just sat in the car holding his plastic bag. I had a burning question that I needed an answer to after reading the report that was given to me. I opened the car door, gave the boy some sweets to eat, along with the driver and headed for the open door. "Hodi" "Hodi," I said as I waited for the familiar, 'Karibu' 'Karibu' response. That done, I walked into the mud floor house. There was a man lying on the floor in a long trench coat, and Pastor was kneeling at the man's side. I walked over to them and knelt down to this skeleton of a man with the same sunken eyes which I remembered so well from the time I came out here to Africa in 1999. "Sir," I said, "I don't want to be disrespectful. I just seek knowledge and understanding, but please can you tell me why, knowing that you had contracted the virus, did you spread it to not only to your wife but also to eleven other women?" He stopped staring at me as the Pastor repeated what I had said. His head turned away from me, and I didn't know if he was upset with me or not. He then slowly turned his head towards me again and said, "Because I don't want to die alone."

It rains quite heavily on the mountain during the 'rainy' season, and the little boy who had been found abandoned developed a very bad chest cold.

The doctors explained to me that it was probably due to exposure, and we did not know how long he had been left outside. The rain was torrential when the night nurse came to my door and woke me up to say she was very concerned about the child's breathing. I left my bedroom, placing on a plastic poncho over my jacket to see how serious the child's condition was.

I could hear the heavy wheezing, and although he was only eighteen months of age, I thought Mark could possibly be suffering from asthma.

I left the nursery, went back into the rain, and shouted for the askari (moran warrior) to get his torch and prepare to go down the mountainside.

It was around 2:00 a.m., and I knew this journey could be dangerous. The quickest way to the dispensary was a steep downward trail with only a hedge to grasp at for support, often was the case that I would be going down to catch the public transport, and I would slip and fall on my butt two or three times before I had reached the main road, but tonight with this heavy rain the trail could be treacherous.

I prayed before the gates closed behind us. Mark was wrapped in a blanket and under the plastic poncho. When we started the descent, the askari was holding my waist with both hands in an effort to not let me fall as he shone the torch on the path. After about five minutes of walking in the heavy rain, he pulled me to a stop, and I turned around to face him. He handed me the torch as he pulled out his simy (long knife like a machete). As the rain poured on to my face, I looked at the Maasai with his simy raised above his head and thought, "Dear God, is this how I die?" No sooner had I thought this, then the Maasai turned on his heels bringing the knife down hard on to a long black snake. He lifted the snake up, now headless, in the torch light and laughed at me. He indicated that I had just walked over it.

We continued our journey to the dispensary. A night porter opened up the dispensary gate and went to awaken the doctor who was on duty that night. We sat on a platform bench and waited, watching the rain pour down. Mark's breathing seemed to be getting worse, and I started to pray my silent prayers to Jesus to please not allow this child to die. The doctor eventually arrived, put the lights on in her room, and we walked in. I un-wrapped Mark from his warm blanket and laid him on the table, and he started to cry. The doctor placed her stethoscope on to his chest and listened intently to his breathing. She went over to a cabinet and pulled out a syringe and some drugs. She asked me to take his top clothes off and lay him on his front. She took hold of a piece of skin below a shoulder blade and stuck the needle in. She slowly poured the contents of the syringe into his back, and she said she would make a bed up for me for the night. In the morning, I would have to admit Mark to the children's ward of the local hospital in Moshi. Thanking her profusely as Mark's breathing had already improved, I went out to speak with the askari and asked him to return up the mountain and ask the night nurse to prepare a bag of clothes for Mark, and some clothes for me out of my room.

We were admitted on to the children's ward of the local hospital the following day, and I caused quite a stir with the African ladies, who had never seen a child being taken care of by an mzungu (European) before. In the morning of my first night at the local hospital, some kind soul had crept under my bed during the night and emptied the contents of my bag, including all Mark's nappies and clothes. Thankfully, I had had the sense to place my purse under my pillow and lay on it, or else that too would have probably disappeared. A carer arrived the following morning, and I had to give her some money to go and purchase supplies to replenish the one's that had been stolen.

I was in the ward with Mark for five days, and during that time, I witnessed five children die, two in the same bed within three hours of each other. I couldn't wait to leave the ward and go home, and I felt desperately unhappy, saddened by what I had seen.

The following day, Mark was his happy cheerful self as he was placed back in to the nursery to be with all of his little friends. The sun was shining, and it was a beautiful day, but I had a really 'heavy' heart that I couldn't shake it off. I went in to my office, and there in the out-tray was a referral from a Chairman of a village who wanted me to go and remove some 'chiggers" from an orphan's foot. I had a pot of tea and decided that a long walk was probably just what the doctor would have ordered.

After I would deliver the food to the villagers, I was then asked if I would help people by removing a parasite called a 'chigger' which is 'flesh eating.' It would bury itself into the skin, and it was most active and painful around 7:00 p.m. in the evening when it would start eating the surrounding skin. I had watched our nurse remove a chigger from a staff members foot and was horrified to see her using a 'pin' that was not sterilized. I had become quite proficient at the removal of these parasites, and with a new pack of razor blades, I started to walk with two askaris to the village where the referral had indicated.

I started to feel much better as I was greeted along the way. People were now much more accepting of me than they had been before as they realized I had no other agenda accept to offer help to the poor and the motherless and fatherless child. We arrived at a house, and there a young woman of about twenty years of age came forward to welcome me to her home.

She took me over to a table that she had prepared outside near some trees and I started to lay out items on the table that I would need like alcoholic wipes and iodine if I happened to crush a parasite and leave the eggs in the hole it had made. I had actually seen chiggers which had turned 'green' under the skin. They must have smelt terribly, and I wondered how much pain the patient must have been in.

"Mama," came a whisper from my left side. I looked up at the Maasai who was pointing to a wooden shed which looked like a goat pen. I watched as the young women removed a padlock from the outside of the door and pulled the door wide open. A skeletal figure came slowly out on bended hands and knees looking around as he slowly entered the sunshine from the dark shed.

"Let me take this in," I thought. I have just watched a young woman remove a large padlock and open a door where a boy was locked inside?!" The two Maasai askaris rushed to the young boy of around fifteen years of age and tried to lift him up to allow his feet to touch the ground, but the child was so thin and weak he couldn't manage it. So the two Maasai lifted him up between them and brought him over to the table and laid him on it.

The boy started whimpering, and he was obviously afraid. He had the most beautiful eyes and eye lashes that I had ever seen. It was as if when they locked on to your eyes he could see right into your soul. I took hold of his hand and tried to comfort him, as I offered him a sandwich from my picnic tin. He was desperately hungry and placed the whole sandwich straight into his mouth. I turned my back to him and looked at his swollen feet. I opened up an alcoholic wipe and started to clean the area. I was aware of the young woman yanking a branch from a tree, and stripping the outer layer from it, but I continued cleaning his big toe which was bulbous with 'chiggers'. As I started the procedure, the boy started to cry, and the women came over to him to beat the boy with the branch. She had peeled the branch to allow the sap to run so that if she made an open wound, it would hurt even more than ever. I turned and asked the askaris to pick up the boy and carry him to our center, and I started to pack everything away. I wagged my finger at the woman, quite at a loss for any Kiswahili words that I might know which would satisfactorily express my anger for what she must have inflicted on this poor child during the last months or even years.

For the following four months after James had come into our care, I did not have a full night's sleep. James was mentally challenged, and each night after eating his evening meal, he would sleep for a few hours and then awaken and go outside crawling on his hands and knees searching in the gravel and grass looking for any particles of food that a child may have dropped. The knock on the door and the same words which I heard for the four months were, "Mama, James is out." I would get out of bed, put on my dressing gown, go outside, pick up James from his knees, and slowly walk him into the kitchen and give him a glass of milk and a jam sandwich.

I would then put him back into his bed, where another 2-3 hours later he would repeat the same sequence. This took four months before his mind told him that he was going to receive three meals per day, but James was a hoarder, and he would take anything that he took a shine too. Thankfully, he always placed his 'booty' in the same blue metal trunk that we had given to him, so if a child shouted "have you seen?" before the sentence was completed someone would announce, "Have you looked in James' trunk?"

When we investigated the case to find out why was this child being starved, we found that he was entitled to a piece of land of around a ¼ of an acre. Apparently the woman had thought that was a good enough reason to starve this mentally disabled child.

James died after living with us for six years. We were told he was an orphan, but surprisingly, we were introduced to his mother at the funeral!

CHAPTER TWELVE
THE PRUNED TREE

I found myself in 'major' prayer mode. Funds had only 'trickled' into our bank account over the last few months, and I just could not understand why. There was always sufficient money for our daily food needs but no extra money to pay the staff wages, and the situation was now dire.

Was this a period of time in a Christians walk which people referred to as 'a wilderness time' when it is really hard to break through into the 'throne room of heaven?' It didn't feel like that to me, so I just prayed for revelation and understanding and more grace to try to understand the situation that I now found myself in.

Five month's had passed and the staff had not received any wages.

I happened to be busy in the nursery changing the nappy of a new baby that had been brought into our care, as I had made it a mandate that no child is ever refused when brought to us. If we were to refuse to accept the child for whatever reason, the child's life could then be severely limited. I looked up and noticed that a shaft of light shone through the window, and highlighted the contour of a young woman in her twenties who I employed as a cleaner in the homes. I noticed that she looked as if she could be pregnant. "Oh, are you expecting a baby?" I asked the young lady. She quickly tried to place a loose shawl around herself and replied, "No." Seeing her embarrassment, I apologized to her for my mistake and carried on with my work. The following day – a

Saturday – the lady in question did not arrive for work and I thought nothing of it until in the late evening, when another staff member quietly asked if she could speak with me in my office. "Yes, of course," I replied, and we walked over together to my room. When the door was firmly closed, tears welled up in her eyes. "Whatever is the matter?" I asked placing an arm around her shoulders. "It's about Rosa" she replied. "Is she sick?" I responded. "She's hemorrhaging heavily. She desperately needs to go to a medical center." She walked away from my grasp and sat down on the chair nearest the desk. "Is she at home?" I asked. "No she's staying at a friend's house." "How far away is that?" I asked. "Not too far," she replied, being somewhat evasive with her answers. "Ok. I'll send a runner for a pick-up truck to come. It has rained quite heavily, so a pick-up with chains on the tyres will be the only vehicle able to get down the narrow road to the center. If you can go to where she is staying and bring her here, I'll get everything arranged." She stood up and hurried out of the room, and I busied myself finding the necessary funds for the transport and the medical expenses.

When Rosa eventually arrived at the children's home being heavily supported by her friend, she looked terribly pale and was obviously in a great deal of pain. As she hugged her stomach, we assisted her into the front seat next to the driver whilst the staff member, and I climbed into the rear of the pick-up truck. We could hear little gasps of pain from Rosa as we drove over the water channels or a ridge in the road, and we quickly climbed over the tailboard when we arrived outside the medical center to help Rosa out of the vehicle.

I paid the necessary funds to open a file at the center and for the doctor's consultation and extra funds for any further drugs or treatment that she may require, and then I walked into the ward to see how Rosa was feeling.

The young-looking doctor informed me that she would be admitted onto the ward for further observation. I left the staff member to care for her personal needs, and the hire vehicle dropped me back at the children's home.

The following day in the late afternoon, our staff member returned from the medical center. Before I could ask how Rosa was doing, she grabbed my hand and pleaded with me to help Rosa. "I don't understand?" I said. "What more can I do? The doctor knows what he is doing, and I'm sure she will be fine. Just some bed rest will sort the problem out," I confidently responded. "Rosa," the staff member said in a hushed whisper, "has gone to a traditional midwife and had an abortion." "What?" I screeched, knowing that anyone found to be assisting in an abortion could be prosecuted and sent to prison for many years. "That's why she is bleeding so heavily," she continued whispering. I walked out the door and hurried to my bedroom.

"WWJD – what would Jesus do! WWJD – what would Jesus do?" The anagram kept going over and over in my mind as I paced up and down my bedroom praying for guidance. Condemnation and guilt quickly made its presence known in my mind as I wondered what would have happened if I hadn't mentioned about the baby. Would it still be safely ensconced in its mother's womb? But why had she done this? As far as I knew, this would have been her first child. I gave the next few hours over to the Lord, collected my handbag, and walked through the door. I spotted the staff member who had given me the news and motioned for her to accompany me through the gate. The fifty minute hike was walked in silence as we trudged ankle deep in mud to the center where Rosa was staying. My mind wandered back to the time I had operated a pregnancy testing center. Teenage pregnancies and abortions were the highest ever recorded in the town where I had lived, and for two years I ran the 'Heartbeat Pregnancy Testing' Center where I offered 'free' pregnancy tests and advice. A friend who helped me run the center came rushing into the office one day, 'high as a kite' and bubbling all over, her mass of curly rich auburn hair bobbing about as she gestured with her hands. "You'll never guess what has just happened to me!" she elatedly gushed. 'I was just buying some fruit from a market stall before coming over here to the center when a woman who was pushing a 'twinney' pushchair stopped by me and said, "Are you the lady who works at the advice center?" to which I replied, "Yes, I am." She then said, "Thank you so much for helping me to see things clearly. I decided not to go ahead and have an abortion, and here are my two beautiful babies. My partner and I are so happy that we made the right decision, and they have brought with them so much love. Thank you," and we chatted for a while and then we said goodbye.' As it happened, we very rarely saw the outcome of a decision someone had made after we had given a positive test result, but this was one such a time and brought great joy for us to know two babies' lives had been saved."

Some month's later, I had just completed a urine test and given the lady the result that her test was positive when she straight away asked me if I could organize for her to undergo an abortion. "Sorry. No", I replied. "You need to make an appointment to see your general practitioner for further advice on this decision." As I was removing my latex gloves and running the tap to wash my hands, I looked over my shoulder and asked the women why she had made such an immediate decision to have an abortion without thinking about it first. She replied, "I can't have a kid and a new sofa which I'm saving up for this year. I'd rather have a new sofa any day than have another kid." I walked her down the steps to the front door and closed the door behind her, put the open sign to closed, and sadly, never opened the center again. When a material object such as a sofa that would wear out or go out of fashion was more important than the life of a child, I was done.

The staff member and I sat down on the platform bench outside of the medical center and removed our 'mud-laden' lead boots and walked barefooted to the ward to see how Rosa was doing. My first question to her was how much blood had she received from a transfusion as by my reckoning she had been bleeding for quite some time. "None," she replied. I walked out the ward to find the doctor. After the initial greeting which is such an integral part of Tanzanian culture, I asked him why he hadn't given Rosa a blood transfusion. "We don't do that procedure here" he replied. "So do I understand this situation correctly? You are quite prepared for this woman just to bleed to death without referring her to a hospital that does offer blood transfusions?" He considered my question and then replied that he would write a referral letter to the general hospital. I walked outside and replaced my heavy footwear and walked to the local market place to find some transport that would take Rosa to the casualty department of the main hospital.

I returned to the hospital with the vehicle, and after the referral letter was given, placed Rosa into the vehicle with her friend and gave her all the money that I had in my purse, but not before getting the 'full SP' on the situation.

It appeared that during the evening hours when everyone was fast asleep, Rosa and one of our security guards were having an illicit love affair, and a baby was the outcome from it.

The following day was a Monday morning, so Coupa and I scraped together what funds we could find to allow me to go into town to see if there was any money placed into our bank account.

On my arrival at the bank, the door was closed. "Dear God" what am I going to do now?" I bemoaned to myself. "I haven't even any change to get back up the mountain." I just stood there on the spot praying. I heard a noise behind me and saw the door opening and the branch manager standing there. Without uttering a word he motioned for me to enter the bank. I hurried forward, and as I went over to get my piece of paper to write my request for withdrawal of funds, I said, "Thank you so much for opening the door for me. I know I have only a very small amount of money in the account but I have to withdraw 10,000/- (approx. $6.00) just for my transport back up the mountain," and I walked over to the cashier at her booth with the completed slip. As she was processing the account on her computer, she suddenly said, "OH", and I looked up at her expectantly. She smiled at me as she said, "Mama, you have just had 1,000,000/= TZ shillings placed into your bank account. (approx $550.00) Utter joy rushed through my veins as I happily withdrew the funds to pay all of the staff wages and knew that, thank God, the tree had been pruned and now life would get back to normal.

CHAPTER THIRTEEN
WORSE CASE IN FORTY YEARS

Two years later life had pretty well settled down, and my daughter and three grandchildren joined me – the youngest being just four years of age – 'just to help out for 1 year,' which actually lasted six years. Some months after their arrival, my youngest son, Marcus, also decided that he would come and join the mission and serve God on the mountain. These were my blessings. When I left the UK, I had no idea if I would ever see my family again, and yet here was God bringing two of my children to live with me. Marcus still lives and serves Light in Africa on a voluntary basis and has married a local girl, Gudilla, who is also the Secretary of Light in Africa and has presented me with three handsome grandsons. Marcus is my 'mighty' prayer warrior and my supporter and encourager when things get a little 'humpty dump.'

The Friday food program and the out-reach dispensary were still continuing. After delivering the food, people would wait for me to arrive at a 'stick shelter' to help them have their 'chiggers' removed or ask for help. I saw my first victim who was suffering from Elephantiasis, and I was amazed at how the human body could react to a bite from a Coastal fly and inflict such damage to a limb. This poor man's leg actually looked like an elephant's leg with its hard shell and dark coloring. Sadly there was nothing anyone could do to help the man.

It had been an exhaustingly long day, and the porters were tidying everything away in the containers that we carried everything in, when we heard heavily labored breathing coming up the steep path. Then this man came through the opening and collapsed full length on to a bench. He was drenched with perspiration and was trying desperately to regain his breath. He had obviously been running hard.

Pastor Alfred spoke to him to find out what the problem was, and the porters were emphatically shaking their heads. I went over and asked what the problem was. "This man has run all the way here to try to catch us before we leave. He has heard that there are a family of five children who are starving to death. The ground has already been dug to receive the youngest one. He's asking if we will go and help these children now" "Of course we will," I said. "The problem is," continued the Pastor, "it will soon be dark and the porters are saying it is too dangerous to be on the mountain during night fall. We have to leave for home now, and where these children live is miles away. They are refusing to go, saying we can come back tomorrow." "No, we can't," I said. "Twelve hours in the lives of severely malnourished children will make all the difference between life and death. If there is a chance we can save these children, we have to go now." After further intense discussion, I persuaded the porters to accompany me, not through the compassion to help these children but because I had promised them three times the amount for their day's wage.

We had been walking for over an hour, and dusk was starting to settle as we arrived at the top of a ridge and looked down into a valley. We could see a small house with wet ground surrounding it and two small children sitting outside. Pastor suggested that he should go down first and look around along with the man who had shown us the way to the house. We stood watching them walk down the valley to where the children were and stooped to go inside the house.

A little while later, the Pastor re-appeared, and we watched as he removed his handkerchief from his pocket and wiped his eyes. I looked at one of the porters and he just shrugged his shoulders, and the Pastor slowly started to walk back up the hill towards us. We didn't say anything until he was ready to speak.

"Prepare yourself for a shock," he choked out, tears starting to run down his cheeks. "I have never seen anything like this, ever".

The porters moved out, and I followed behind everyone. I approached the two small children who were sitting outside, and I bobbed down to their height and held some sweets out in the palm of my hand, whilst the Pastor and the porters went into the small house. The children walked towards the sweets on their knees and on their elbows. When a hand was extended, I could see that they were full of 'chiggers,' and they couldn't place their feet on the ground due to the swelling from this dastardly parasite.

We looked down the path as the light was failing and could just see a woman walking very slowly towards us. Pastor Alfred was already motivating the porters to empty the containers to look for any rice or any food of any kind that we could give to the children. I always had food left in my lunch box as with the heat I found it difficult to eat. In the first three months of living on the mountain, I had lost two stone (28lbs). He then went over to talk to the woman. I heard his voice rise in anger as he admonished her for allowing the children to suffer with the parasite without helping them, and I walked over to them and could see her feet were also full of 'chiggers'. I failed to understand why she would allow very young children to suffer such pain and discomfort and not do anything to help them. A bag of rice had split open, and a porter was gleaning as much of the rice as he could from the backpack and placing it in an empty plastic bag. The man who had so faithfully ran to inform me and to show us the way to where these children were living was called over, and I thanked him for being such a 'good Samaritan'. After I had surveyed all of these pitiful little children, especially the youngest who was extremely malnourished and weak, I gave the man some money to run to a farm and purchase some milk in one of our empty water bottles and some food stuff, and I asked the man to ensure the local ten cell leader and the

Chairman of the village was here at 10:00 a.m. in the morning. He dashed off again holding the money like an Olympic sprinter holding on to a prized baton, and we prepared to leave in the dark knowing the children were going to receive some food.

The following day, we spoke to the leaders of the village who wrote a letter for LIA to hand to the social welfare department, and we carried the children to the center. I hired a vehicle to take the children, first to the social welfare department, who said it was the worst case that that they had seen in forty years, and then on to the hospital for the removal of the 'chiggers,' which were even under the children's fingernails. On our way back to the center, we were asked by the social welfare department to accommodate four more children who were all boys of four years of age from another home which only cared for babies up to the age of four years. So in one weekend, nine more children joined our ever growing family.

As the family of five children could still have some eggs of the chiggers, we had to place them in isolation so as not to pass the parasite on to our other children. As the children had lived a very sheltered and isolated life, when ever one of our 'curious' children came to the door to make friends with them, they would scream the place down, until we came and moved the child from the doorway. We left the door open so that the children could see into the courtyard and watch the children playing on the swings outside. We watched and observed as a metamorphism began to take place, one by one as their feet and hands began to heal the children walked upright out of the door and went to join the children in play. After six weeks of healing time, I asked the oldest boy of eight years of age if he would like to go to the local school with the other children. He told us that he had never been to school and that he really wanted to attend a school with the other children.

I visited the local Primary school but the headmistress was unable to hold a conversation in English with me even though one of the exams the children have to pass to go to Secondary school is in English.

I left the school, and returned with Pastor Alfred to interpret for me. I explained the situation that Donald had never attended school and that he was unsure of himself and self conscious around other children and asked would she please ask her staff not to beat the boy as he had just undergone a traumatic episode in his young life. She agreed that she would pass my comments on to her staff members.

Excitedly, Donald tried on his new school uniform, and all day Sunday, he had his back pack on with his exercise books in. He would sit on his bed and arrange and re-arrange all of his new books and pencils that he would need for the following day. I waved them all off to school like a mother hen with her chicks and waited for their return to find out how Donald had enjoyed school. The children ran into my office and quickly explained to me that Donald had been beaten with a stick on his hands. Utterly shocked, I recalled the state his hands had been in from the removal of the 'chiggers' – 'red raw'.

I went to find him, and he was in the dormitory sitting on his bed crying. What could I possibly say to this poor child to comfort him? Only a hug and to be taken into the kitchen for milk and a jam sandwich brought him back to his old self as the other children watched from the kitchen door.

Donald and the children left for school the following day, and when Pastor Alfred arrived, I asked him to accompany me once again to the school to speak with the teachers again. In simple terms, I tried to explain that being a child who was eight years of age and just starting Primary school was hard enough in itself, but to beat him for not knowing the answer to a question was just not fair on the child. He would start to hate to come to school. The Headmistress agreed with me, and I thought perhaps this would be the last time that I would have to come to the school over this issue. Three weeks later the children ran through the gate in a hurry to tell me the latest news about Donald. He had been severely beaten by a teacher for not having his school books. The children had witnessed him burying them all in the school playground. "Where is he?" I demanded from the children.

"He didn't come with us," one of them replied. Just before I went to organize the search party, Donald walked slowly through the gate with his head down, and I herded him straight into the office. "Would you like to tell me what has happened today?" He burst into tears. After he calmed down, I asked him why he had buried his school books in the school yard. "Because I would rather be beaten for not having my school books than beaten and laughed at for not knowing the answer," and he burst into another flood of tears.

That was the last day that Donald attended that school. He was transferred to a school in Moshi with a 'no beating policy" called Mount Kilimanjaro School, whose curriculum is from Cambridge University. Donald is now in his twenties and has gained "B"s in Biology and has the ability to become a doctor if he so chooses.

CHAPTER FOURTEEN
WORKING WITH THE KILIMANJARO MAASAI

Six months after my arrival on the mountain, I received a delegation of Maasai elders who had travelled some distance to visit with me.

Their request was that I should go and build a children's home in their village. I apologized and said that was not possible unless God told me to go build a children's home in their village. "But," I carried on, "if you have children who are suffering, then what I can offer you is to come into your village once a month to offer you a medical out-reach program."

That was the beginning of a long relationship working with the Maasai of Kilimanjaro.

Besides involving the services of a local doctor, and purchasing the necessary drugs, I would also take with me a sack of rice usually for distribution to the Maasai's many wives and children. I never gave food to the Maasai morans (warriors) as they had all the power and the money to purchase food. They would kill a cow outside of the village, and all the morans would eat the steak and leave the offal for the women and children.

My biggest 'mental headache' was in trying to understand the traditional ways of this tribe which hadn't changed it's 'thought patterns' in generations and a lot of bad practices still existed.

The Maasai have chosen to have little exposure to education, preferring their children as young as seven years of age to herd the cows and goats and not attend school.

The present Government has made huge strides in trying to change this situation and using local leaders to enforce the parents to send their children to school. It is now common to see the Maasai using mobile phones and purchasing cars and motorbikes, and I have even seen a Maasai mama riding a bicycle! Progress indeed.

The Maasai are pastoralists and will walk many days looking for grass for their animals to eat. They also indulge in polygamous marriages, with some Maasai morans (warriors) having 5-6 wives. Each wife is responsible for building her own boma (house made of sticks and cow dung) inside her husband's encampment, and it is her job to milk the cows and care for her many children. Like their neighbors, the Chagga's living on Mount Kilimanjaro, the Maasai mama, on delivery of her first child, loses her own identity and becomes known as the mother of the first named child, i.e. Mama Valance or Mama Martha. The husband is also referred to as Baba Valance or Baba Martha and not by the name that was given to him at birth.

The Maasai are a noble tribe, and the rituals and the brotherhood of the warriors mean everything to their lifestyle. The morans will shoot an arrow into the artery of a cow and draw its blood then mix it with milk and drink it, plugging up the hole that the arrow has made with mud. They believe that when they drink the animal's blood, they are also obtaining the strength from that animal. Whenever we operate a seminar on the HIV/AIDS virus and the use of condoms, we always have to ensure the men are separated from the women, and the women are being taught in their own age groups. Only when these procedures have been followed can we then try to educate them into a different way of thinking to protect them from diseases.

Cows to the Maasai morans are their status symbol; the more cows and goats one has, the more you rise in the 'pecking order' of the tribe. The animals, it would appear, are even more important to some Maasai than wives and children.

When a famine hit the village and the children were suffering from hunger, I made a concerted effort to visit the Maasai with the largest herd of cows and goats.

"Hello sir," I started my introduction with an air of respect to this very wealthy Maasai moran warrior, who happened to be standing on one leg, surrounded by his vast herd of cattle. "I have just finished a dispensary in your village, and the doctor has noticed a lot of the children he has seen today are becoming malnourished. I can see that you are such an important man having such a large herd of cattle. Would you give me a cow so that I can feed the children and give them some protein in their diet?" "No," came back the reply. "Why not?" I ventured to ask. "Because, if I give you a cow today you will come back again and ask me for another cow," and soon I would have no cows left." "OK sir, if you won't give me a cow today, will you give me a goat to feed the children? "No," came back the forceful response. Not to be deterred, I persisted. "If I make a promise to you that I will only ever ask you for one cow and just one goat, will you give them to me to enable me to feed the children?" "No. No cows and no goats" he was now standing on two legs and looking quite adamant that nothing was going to be taken from his herd. "Tell me, sir. Do you consider yourself to be a 'good' Christian?" (All Maasai profess to be either Catholics or Lutherans never a Muslim due to the way the Muslims slaughter their animals.) "I am a good man. I go to church," he replied, and before I could give my two cents worth of good advice on being a responsible Christian and caring for the needs of others, he whistled to his dog and moved off, looking back at me just once with a look that was quite indescribable as I stood rooted to the spot watching him move away with his vast herd as dust from the hooves of the cattle swirled around me.

I had been privileged to be invited to a 'change – over ceremony' which occurs when the circumcised brotherhood moves to the next level of maturity in their life cycle. (Suggested reading - The World of a Maasai Warrior, by Tepilit Ole Saitoti) With a doctor and a group of

Maasai carrying our trunks full of medical drugs, we started to walk to where the ceremony was being held somewhere in a remote field to hold a medical dispensary for the many expected Maasai guests who had walked for many a day just to be present at this momentous occasion.

After about a five kilometer walk, I started to behave like a child in the back seat of a car, "Are we there yet?" I asked, and one of the Maasai would point a finger and say, "You see that acacia tree over there? When we reach that tree, we are there," and of course we weren't. "When we reach the river bed, then we're there," and of course we weren't. I told them, "Thank you for today. I have really learnt a lot, and that is to never again ask a Maasai 'how far is it', because it might not be far for you as you walk miles each day, but for a wazungu with soft feet, I am totally exhausted before I have even started the day's dispensary." This is the philosophy of how the tour companies manage to get the tourist to summit Mount Kilimanjaro.

The Maasai had gathered from all over Uganda, Kenya, and Tanzania for this very important ceremony. And it all had to do with the circumcision group each Maasai belonged to according to the time they were circumcised.

I was very impressed that it was so un-commercialized. Two tarpaulin tents had been erected: one for food and one for drinks. If that had been for the wazungu's (Europeans), it would have been like a fairground, a money making commercial enterprise.

I witnessed the 'Holy Cow' being suffocated. There were some concerns by the eldership that the cow had tried to break free instead of being executed peacefully, and that could mean a 'bad omen,' but other elders disagreed that it was natural to fight for life.

I was also privy to a man being beaten by four men for some misdemeanor, who was then dragged over to where we had set up 'our stall' underneath a tree for shade, and the man was bodily dropped in front of the doctor to heal his wounds. The doctor prescribed for well over 200 patients that day, and then we had to walk the return journey home. My blistered feet were 'killing' me and my 'hot' water shower from a bucket was a pure undulated luxury as I poured it over my head. Thank goodness another exciting day was over.

The facility that we used when working in the Maasai village where the elders had asked for help, was a small room next to the cow shed. I would employ a local doctor for the day to help these people with their medical problems as well as distribute the rice.

There were many patients waiting to see the doctor when we arrived this one particular day. And as the doctor was seeing his first patients, I once again became the 'queue manager'. The mama's might have arrived early with a sick child to await our arrival, and then a Maasai moran would just push to the front and expect to be seen next. It wasn't long before the Maasai morans were calling me by another name, 'kali sana mama' meaning 'stern mama'. The mama's would laugh as I would push a warrior to the back of the queue and make him wait his turn to see the doctor, something that the mama's would never dare do for fear of being beaten, but because of my 'grey' hair I got away with quite a lot. Their culture demands respect for the elderly.

I heard the doctor shouting for me to come and see a child. I walked in the room and saw he had a small girl lying across his lap. When I came closer, he opened her legs to reveal that she had been circumcised. I was flooded with emotions as I tried to comprehend the horror that this young child of eighteen months must have gone through. "The child has to have an emergency operation straight away," the doctor said. "It is taking her forty minutes to pass urine due to a fistula growing over the opening." "When did they perform the 'cut' on this child?" I asked close to tears. "I'm guessing when she was about twelve months of age," the doctor replied. I always thought it was done after the first menstrual cycle as a 'rite of passage,' or a moran warrior would demand it before he married a young girl. I was trying to search for reasons in my mind as to why they would do this to such a young child. "Can't answer that one," the doctor replied as he passed the child over to her mother to hold.

I left the room totally shocked at the barbarity of it all and once again, wondered what had I gotten myself in to. I just wanted to walk away, and leave all these horrible cruel things that happen to young children behind me. I continued to walk away from the dispensary deep in thought and emotions.

I heard noises behind me and turned around, I was like the Pied Piper of Hamelin being followed by all of these Maasai children running after me. I carried on walking trying to put some distance between me and the dispensary. Eventually, I sat down on a hill and placed my head in my arms as I didn't want the children to see me in tears. The girls started to play with my hair and the boys with the shoelaces of my boots that I wore in the bush, but I could have screamed at them to just leave me alone. Then the peace that passes all understanding flowed over me, and I heard the 'small inner voice' say, "Let it out. Let it all out." I looked up and wondered what the future held for all of these young girls. Possibly married by the age of twelve to fourteen and having a baby by the age of fifteen. It would be a case of a child having a child. And with the moran warriors being a brotherhood, it was open season for anyone to take the girl. It is alleged that when a Maasai walks off to find grass for his cows and he returns home to find a spear stuck in the ground in front of his boma (house) that he cannot go in until the Maasai who is with his wife comes out and removes his spear and walks away. Then the husband can go into his home.

A plan was forming in my mind, and I returned to talk to the doctor who was busy writing out the referral letter to the hospital requesting surgery on the child. After I had formulated the plan and he had agreed to it, he left the room to find the Chairman of the village for a call to be put out for all of the women in the village to be at the dispensary within the next hour.

One hour later, all of the women had gathered in a circle including the women who would have performed the 'cut' on the child. Boy, did I let my feelings out! The doctor interpreting for me had a hard job keeping up with me. When I raised my voice, he raised his voice, and we were together as one voice in this outpouring of emotions. I told them, "I have been coming to this village all these years at great expense. I have fed them. I have paid for operations when they were sick, and purchased malaria drugs when they had malaria. I have paid school fee's so thir children would be able to access education. I have done everything humanly possible to help this village, and you go and do this to this little child. Well that is it! The doctor and I are packing all the medicines away, and we are leaving and not coming back until this vile practice stops." And with that, we walked away and started to pack all of our trunks with the unused drugs. As we walked down the road, mama's were following us and crying and begging us to go back. But my mind was made up. I had to do something to stop this inhuman practice. A pick-up truck stopped for us, and the doctor climbed into the rear whilst I passed him the trunks. As I climbed on the tailboard, the mama's got hold of my legs and were trying to pull me so that I couldn't get into the truck. The doctor stood up and took hold of both my hands, and by sheer force, pulled me into the truck. As the truck pulled away, he shouted to the mama's, "Stop the FGM (Female Genital Mutilation) and we will come back," and the truck sped away.

Four months later, the group of elders asked for an interview with me at our center, and when I arrived into the dining room, I was warmly greeted, with many "shikamoo's mama," and then I was very proudly handed a letter.

It had been written in English, and the leader explained to my interpreter that they had asked a school teacher to write it to me. I read the letter and asked them, "but how do I know that this is true?" I was then informed that everyone was so upset when the doctor and I left, and when they realized that the village would be getting no more help whilst they continued with the FGM practice, a meeting of the village was called for it all to be discussed, and the meeting had agreed that they would take the ceremonial 'cutting' knife and pack clay all around it, and they would perform a 'rolling away' ceremony and stop the practice for a total of six years. If no disaster struck the village during this time, then they would continue not to 'cut,' but if anything did happen to the village during this six year period, then the practice would be re-introduced. I then agreed to go back to the village and hold more dispensaries and give more food assistance.

After this meeting, we followed through by taking a generator with a television and video, and we showed the Maasai morans the video of a women being circumcised and what they had to endure, and they all got up and ran out of the room, some actually vomiting. I think we got the message across.

The little girl has since had a further three operations that Light in Africa has paid for.

It has been eleven years since this incident happened, and I recently spoke to the Chairman of the village as to the status quo of circumcision. "Was the village still 'cutting' young girls" I asked. "No," he responded, "since I made it quite clear that the village would receive no further help if they continued the practice, and since the 'rolling away' ceremony had been initiated, no further 'cuts' on girls had been made."

CHAPTER FIFTEEN
CHILD BRIDE

I was preparing to leave for a tour of the USA, with a window of about one hour, before the transport would arrive and take me to the airport, when mama Coupa came into my room and informed me that I had a Social Worker wanting to see me in the office. "Coupa, I can't. You'll have to deal with her. I have to get ready the car will be here soon." She turned on her heels and self-importantly said, "You'll want to see this one," and left. I looked at my watch and thought I could just spare ten minutes, but that would mean my desk didn't get tidied, and Coupa will have to manage that job! The local district social worker was waiting for me with a young Maasai girl close by her side, and she asked if the girl could stay at the home for her protection as she had just been circumcised and whilst lying there bleeding, she had heard her father take the 'bride price' for her to be married to an eighty year old man as his eighth wife. As soon as she could, she had ran away from the village. The girl was twelve years of age.

I called for the vehicle to come over earlier and take the girl to the doctor that we work with to ensure there was no infection, and I asked the social worker what cause of action she had taken. "I really don't get much support from the local agencies," she replied, "even though the Government has banned the practice. The father and the proposed husband is in the cells at present, but I don't think it will be long before they are released."

On my return from the States, I intensified our seminars by producing a drama with our volunteers and visiting many schools in an effort to stop this practice.

A young medical volunteer was helping the doctor to re-pack all the un-used medicines away in to the medical trunks when I decided I would hand out some sweets to some Maasai children. Insisting that all the children must make a line before I would distribute the sweets so that 'little legs' would not get trampled on, I started to pass out the sweets when this pretty Maasai woman came and stood next to me and showed me her baby.

One look at the child, and I shouted loudly for the doctor to come immediately. The baby's lips and fingernails were blue. I didn't need a doctor to tell me this baby had a heart condition after the experience that I had had with my own daughter. He rushed out of his room, took one look at the child and said 'another emergency.'

He explained as quickly as possible to the mother that she must fetch her husband and the village leader and tell them the child must go to hospital "Haraka sana" (right now). With the help of the volunteer, we hurriedly packed everything into the car, put the mother and child in to the back, collected one of our carers from the home and drove straight to the hospital.

It was around lunchtime of the following day, when I arrived at the hospital to check how the baby was doing. Coming through the hospital gate was the mother and the carer. I sensed straight away that the baby was already in the mortuary. The carer explained to me what had happened. In the night, the baby had died, but due to the wailing noises that the Maasai make when someone dies, she had not been told until this morning. "I've paid the mortuary fee with the money that you gave me," the carer said ensuring everything had been properly taken care of. I thanked her and looked around for a taxi. I found one and we all got into the taxi, and I gave directions to the Maasai village. The mother started to cry, and the taxi driver asked me what she was crying for. I explained that her baby son had died.

He pulled the taxi to the side of the road, and switched the engine off. Bewildered by his action, the driver turned in his seat to face me. "I'm not going anywhere near her village with this taxi," he said. "Do you know what they will do to me for taking her back and especially to her because she has lost the baby? They will beat us," he said. "Of course they won't beat us," I said indignantly. "I have been working with the Maasai for a long time now. They will understand that the baby has died of a congenital defect." "We shall be beaten if we go," he insisted. I spoke to the carer and she confirmed that she had heard of such things as this. "Best drive us up the mountain to our center, and then I will sort the matter out from there," I instructed the driver.

On arrival at the center, I sent a Maasai 'runner' back to the village to ask for the Chairman and the women's husband to come to the center to see me. They arrived the next day, and after telling them about the baby's death, I made them promise me that on returning to the village the woman would not be beaten, to which they agreed, and the woman left with them.

The burial of the baby was four days later, and the family asked me if I would pay for the pick-up truck to go and collect the baby's body from the mortuary and pay for the coffin, which I did. Another problem had arisen, and that was the local Pastor was refusing to bury the baby because it hadn't been baptized. However, the Pastor had a mind change when Pastor Alfred said he would step in and perform the service.

When the proceedings started, I was asked by the Chairman of the village if I would say a few words, and I tried to educate all the villagers that were present to the fact that this little baby had been born with a heart defect, and that the baby would never have grown up to become a strong worrier because there was no hospital in Tanzania that performed heart operations for his heart to have been repaired, so Jesus has taken the baby to be at home with Him, and it is definitely not the fault of the father or of the mother, then the service continued.

Over the next few days, I had no peace about the young mother and decided I would go to the village even though we were not operating a dispensary. On my arrival, the mama's gathered around me, and I asked them if they would bring me the Maasai mama who had lost her first baby. They replied that they couldn't do that because she had been badly beaten and was now living back home with her parents.

I then asked a young Maasai boy to go and ask the Chairman of the village and the father to come to see me, and if necessary I would wait in the village the whole night until they came and faced me.

When they both arrived, I confronted them that I didn't think I could trust either of them again, because in my home they had both promised me that the woman would not be beaten, and today I learn that she has been and is no longer in the village. "Poly sana" (sorry) both of them said, and I left the village.

I thought deep and hard about this situation, and I decided that only exposure to another way, a different way, could possibly change the traditional way that had been passed down by generations of beating children and women, so I invited Raymond – the deceased baby's father -to come and work for me as a security guard and watch how we deal with children's behavior, either with counseling them twice about their unacceptable behavior, or asking them on the third occasion if they would like to assist the staff in cleaning the toilets for a month. They really take me up on this offer and good behavior ensues.

Raymond has been working as a security guard for Light in Africa for over eleven years now and is one of our best and bravest of guards, and he assures me he doesn't beat the gift that God has given him of a new son. I pray that it is true.

CHAPTER SIXTEEN
A WHITE BEAD AND A DELIVERY

My mobile phone rang early one morning, and it was my daughter –in-law Gudilla asking me if I would drive a child to hospital. "What's happened?" I asked. "Last night, our carer was washing little Rachael's neck when she spotted something white down her ear canal. I took her to a dispensary last night, but unfortunately the doctor has only managed to push it further down the canal and now Rachael will require it to be surgically removed at the hospital." "OK, pack the hospital bag. I'll collect her within the hour," I responded.

We arrived early at the hospital and managed to see an ENT specialist who booked Rachael in for afternoon surgery.

As I sat on a hospital bed waiting for Rachael to be returned from the operating theater, I noticed a traditionally dressed Maasai woman going from bed to bed begging for food. She appeared to have had a tracheotomy fitted in her throat. When she approached me, she pushed a plastic plate towards me. I rummaged in my bag and found a small packet of biscuits which I placed on the plate. She smiled and moved on to the next bed.

The doctor appeared and came over to me and placed a small, white bead into my hand that he had extracted from Rachael's ear.

After thanking him, I asked him about the Maasai woman who was 'begging' for food on the ward. The story he told me was a Good

Samaritan had dropped the woman off late one night in a vehicle and driven off leaving the woman outside the gates gasping for breath. From what they had learned from the woman, she had taken a beating from her husband and probably one beat mark had hit her throat resulting in her windpipe swelling up. The doctor had been called and, he had performed an emergency tracheotomy. The woman had been at the hospital for over a month now, and she had received no visitors. As the hospital relied on relatives to bring food in for patients, the woman was only receiving some porridge or ugali (flour and water) and some beans from the hospital kitchen. Consequently, the woman needed to eat more food and was going bed to bed asking for supplements to the hospitals food. This story saddened me that the woman would be abandoned and no one would come forward to pay her hospital bill, I made the suggestion to the doctor that I would approach the Chairman of Light in Africa – who himself is a Maasai - who could visit and communicate with the woman and find out which area she came from and how we could help her. The doctor readily agreed with my suggestion and Rachael came on to the ward being wheeled on a stretcher still fast asleep.

After the Chairman of LIA had visited the woman in hospital and found out that her tribe lived close by one of the National Parks, a long way away. She also confirmed that her husband had badly beaten her, and a man with a car had dropped her off at the hospital. A week after the visit by our Chairman to see the lady, I received two visitors. One was the hospital doctor who had removed Rachael's white bead, and he was accompanied by another doctor. He asked me if the Maasai lady could come and stay at my home for around a month until her 'trachea' was removed as she was taking up bed space. I agreed on condition that LIA didn't pick up the hospital bill for the surgeries, to which he readily agreed.

Anna was a very quite lady and soon busied herself around the house cleaning and washing clothes. When she spotted our nurse arriving, she confided to her that she was pregnant. After a month Anna returned to the hospital to have her 'tracki' removed and came back to my home to live until after the baby was born. LIA's doctor said a home delivery would be fine as this was to be her second baby (her mother in the village was caring for her first child).

There was a slight tap tapping on my bedroom window, and I turned to switch the bedside light on, and draw the curtains to see who it was.

One of the askaris (security) shone his torch on to his face to enable me to see him. "Anna mama. Baby coming" he said, pointing his arm with the torch shining over towards the tree's in the garden. I let the curtains fall back into place and hurriedly dressed. Unlocking the front door and descending the four balcony steps, I could see that all three askaris were shining the torch on Anna who was clinging to a tree. They moved forward to hold her and bring her into the house. They sat her down on a chair whilst I phoned for the doctor to come and perform the delivery. I then went to place a plastic sheets on my granddaughter's vacant bed and make Anna a cup of tea. She didn't appear to be in pain, at least there was no expression of it, and after ensuring she was comfortable on the bed, I went into the bathroom to have a wash and brush my teeth. With a mouthful of toothpaste, I stopped the brushing action to listen to a sound emanating from the bedroom. It was a long primeval moan, and I realized that it sounded like Anna was pushing. I dropped the toothbrush into the sink, quickly wiped my mouth of the toothpaste and ran into the bedroom. The baby was crowning, and as I moved forward, the baby just 'plopped' into my outstretched hands. Totally shocked, I just held the baby. I had never been on this end of a delivery before. "What do I do next," I thought, panic starting to set in, as I gently laid the baby on to her mother's stomach. "I must tie the cord off. Time is of the essence," I thought, as I quickly washed my hands under the cold water tap and soaped up. I took a deep breath, prayed a prayer, and went into the kitchen. I pulled out a sharp knife from the knife block, opened a kitchen draw, and rooted around in it until I found some string. I pulled on the string, and it came apart in my hand. That's no good," I thought and threw the string back in to the draw. I looked frantically around wondering if the baby was breathing its last breath, when I spotted hanging on the back of the door, a child's plastic apron which had a green nylon cord for a neck band. I took the apron down from the peg, cut the ribbon off both ends, folded it in half, cut it, and rushed back into the bedroom holding the knife in one hand and the green ribbon in the other. "Oh heck," where do I tie it off on this cord? Is it an inch from the body or two: I couldn't remember. I tied the first piece of nylon cord and then the second piece. The baby was crying, and I thought that this must be a good sign. As I held the knife between the two pieces of green nylon cord, it suddenly hit me that I hadn't sterilized the knife or anything for that matter. Praying a prayer for grace and mercy for me and protection for the baby and mother, I cut the cord and handed the baby to its mother.

When the doctor eventually dashed through the front door, it was all over. The mother and baby had been bathed, and the baby was wearing a white baby gown. "Ongera sana mama," said the doctor, "congratulations on your first delivery," he said quite proudly.

Anna named the baby Lightness Lynn, and being escorted by our Maasai Chairman and another Maasai back to her village, the chairman thought that it would be appropriate for the mother to take her husband a goat as a peace offering.

I totally fail to understand the workings and the 'mind set' of the Maasai tribe. For goodness sake, the man had beaten his wife nearly to death, and I'm paying for a goat for her husband to appease him? I just don't get it!

CHAPTER SEVENTEEN
DONT ASSUME

Light in Africa is very much a 'grass roots' organization as we not only provide all the necessary ingredients to promote physical and spiritual wellbeing for all of the children in our care, but we also endeavor to help the local communities where we live with out-reach programs which include medical dispensaries into the bush, food kitchens (on any given day, we prepare over 1,000 meals), and seminars on relevant issues like the prevention of the HIV/AIDS virus, Female Genital Mutilation, and contraceptive issues.

Prior to the Kenyan election disturbances between the tribes, LIA was involved in trying to bring education and medical health to a Maasai village that reached out and asked Light in Africa for help.

About 40 kilometers from the border which separates Tanzania from Kenya, we made our presence known in this small Maasai village by building a settlement of round houses (manyattas) which our many volunteers would live in and help the Maasai community in many functional tangible ways. Each round house could sleep two people and were constructed of sticks and cow dung/clay. They looked very attractive with their painted walls and offered our volunteers a unique experience to live and work with the nomadic Maasai. Whilst in the village, we trained the Maasai mama's on hygiene, cooking preparation, preparing and washing bed sheets and mosquito nets. They were ready for our arrival into the village for which they were paid a wage for their work. This was based on a rota which allowed all the village women to participate and learn new life skills and earn some much needed funds to allow them to feed their many children. A Maasai moran can have as many as 4-6 wives and many children, and if he should contract the virus it spreads quickly through the wives and newborns and can have a devastating effect on their families and communities.

I had planned a full program for our next intake of volunteers, and we eventually arrived dusty and dirty after an all-day drive, passing thousands of banana trees on the Tanzanian side then travelling through the check-point border into Kenya and seeing only a few banana trees planted on the mountain on the Kenyan side. It was a stark reminder that planting for the future was paramount for the next generations, survival.

We already have been informed by scientists who have been monitoring the amount of snow and glaciers on Mount Kilimanjaro that they predict all the ice fields will disappear in a few years due to global warming. Sadly, only a small percentage of Tanzanians own cars and refrigerators compared to their wealthy counter-parts overseas where the majority of homes may have one, two or more appliances.

We arrived at the settlement and were delighted that the mama's had placed clean sheets on the single beds and were all prepared for our arrival. We had purchased all the food we would be using over the next few days, stopping en-route to purchase the stalks of green bananas which are part of the staple diet that would be used when the volunteers and the Maasai mama's prepared the food at the Food Kitchen along with the live chickens and fish that we would require.

The training appeared to be working well, as we tried hard to bring education into this remote village.

I had planned a four day trip which would include providing a medical dispensary, a food kitchen and some class teaching, and for my part a meeting with the village elders, to talk about stopping the practice of Female Genital Mutilation. FGM, which is so pandemic with the Maasai tribe, is a 'rite of passage' for a girl to marry even at twelve years of age.

The facilities in the camp were pretty basic with a drop pit latrine, a bucket of water for the shower, and an outside cooking facility. At night when the bonfire was lit, everyone would gather around and enjoy the telling of stories of what had happened throughout the day under a pitch black canopy with a backdrop of diamond studied stars illuminating the night sky. It was a very peaceful time as we sat and wondered if elephants would pass by our camp the following morning as we were taking breakfast.

The following day, as the group followed the program of events, I was escorted over to a boma which was full of Maasai morans. The place was small and dark and made of the usual easy to find ingredients of sticks and cow dung. I could just walk through the doorway erect, but for the Maasai who were all over 6' tall, they had to double over to get through the door.

When all the customary greetings were made through my interpreter, I started the dialogue by saying that these esteemed men could ask me absolutely anything about any subject and I would gladly answer any questions truthfully that they may have and have always wanted to know the answer to. They wouldn't upset me, they wouldn't offend me, and I wouldn't be embarrassed as I had been a wife, a mother, and was now a grandmother, so I had vast experience about many issues that I would like to discuss with them, and later I would like them to agree to attend a seminar which our nurse was going to give on the use of the condom. I could sense there was some resistance to this suggestion, so before I could get to the 'nitty gritty' on the delicate issue of FGM (as I was deliberately targeting the males as it was they who were paying the 'brides price' to the parents and demanding the girls be cut), I had to find a way to bring them around to my way of thinking if I was to gain their trust.

My opening gambit was on education. "Is it correct," I asked the men who sat in their colourful shukas staring at this grey haired women who really had no right to be mixing with them as men and women were separated and the men didn't even eat with the women, 'That the Maasai once owned the best grazing lands but now they are subjected to lands which have been signed away from them due to lack of education and understanding, and now only owned poor unproductive land with little grass to feed their cattle on?" That question burst the flood gates wide open as one after another the men started talking to each other about the question posed. My interpreter had no chance to tell me what was being said with the noise was getting louder and louder as past hurts and family issues were raised and that was just my first question! I could see I was going to be in that confined place for hours, talking, perspiring, drinking bottled water, but I felt it would be well worth it if I could try to make them understand that the practice of FGM can be dangerous for the women when they are giving birth, and in another area we were working in, it was estimated that as many as 60% of the women were dying in childbirth.

After that question had been exhausted, I asked a further provocative question. "From my understanding and observation, I can see that a lot of people make money out of the noble Maasai culture except the Maasai themselves? Why is that?" The interpreter was asked by one Maasai, "What does the mzungu (European) mean?" "Well," I said, "let's look at the shukas (piece of material the Maasai wear) that you are wearing. Each colour that you wear represents the circumcision group that you are part of in the brotherhood, and the women also wear different colours for their status, single girls, married women, or elder women. These shukas are all sold to the tourist and to hotels to promote their image, and a lot of money is made by different businesses. Take the many oil paintings you see being sold by the road side. They are being produced representing different practices that the Maasai are involved in like the jumping high from a standing position that you are all very good at, but I have yet to meet a Maasai artisan who actually paints these pictures? You use the calabash for keeping milk in for the babies. Other people decorate them and sell them. Everyone, it appears to me, makes money out of the Maasai proud culture but the Maasai themselves. Do the Maasai own the factories that make the shukas or does someone who is not a Maasai manufacture them?"

After further intense discussion about 'how does the wazungu know all these things," I brought this discussion to a close by saying, "Gentlemen, this all boils down to one thing: lack of education. You choose not to send your children to school, preferring for them to go and herd the cattle instead, but if I could possibly give you an example in mine and other countries, cultures, it is absolutely essential for our children to attend schools and learn because you are making an investment, like purchasing cows for the future, if your children are educated. Let's look at the volunteers who are with me today in your village. The majority of them are medical students, and they will still go to school for at least another 4-5 years. But, when they become doctors, they will earn a lot of money and the family will benefit from their investment of education in their sons and daughters." Many questions followed as if a veil had been drawn back to reveal something that they had not previously seen or understood. My interpreter was immersed in the conversation for a long time, explaining to the Maasai about how his parents had made him attend school, how he had finished his primary and secondary education, and now had a good job which brought him in a steady income whereby he was able to support his younger siblings through school and support his parents. After a good twenty minutes of me just sitting there in this sweltering mud hut listening to all this noise, I thought it was time to 'hit the nail on the head.' "Gentlemen," I said - one must always show respect to a Maasai" - "please discuss these questions that I have raised between yourselves later, and if you would like to discuss further then we can have a another meeting tomorrow, but I have a very important issue that is very close to my heart that I would like to speak with you about. It's regarding the practice of 'cutting' and marrying girls as young as twelve years of age." Silence prevailed, followed by stern looks in my direction. "Oh boy. I've gone too far now," I thought. I carried on none the less now that I had their full, undivided attention. "Have you seen how the wazungu's, when they walk down the street, the man and the women hold hands and are very close to each other?" One younger than the other Maasai nodded his head, so I took this as a lead to carry on. "Well when you ask for your future wife to be 'cut' before you will marry her you are cutting off her passion!" Quiet whispering followed the interpretation. One brave heart asked me what I meant. I then went into the subject matter a little deeper. "When you have sex with your wife, she doesn't respond. She just lays there because you have cut off a most important part of her body because you believe it will stop her running off with other men, even though you yourselves are all part of a brotherhood and you share the women!

Heads grew closer together in low murmurings as the question was discussed. I then was asked the first question that was posed to me directly: Had I been cut before I was married? "No," I said. "My husband didn't want a women who was not responsive to his advances otherwise all he would have in his bed was the equivalent to a piece of meat! We both wanted shared intimacy that was enjoyable to both parties." I think at this point some fuses burst open in their minds as I was asked some very personal questions after that, and I answered them as directly as I could from my personal experience. We had now been in discussion for over three hours (the Maasai elders can sit under a tree all day and just discuss one subject and at the end of the day have no conclusion or compromise. They just love to sit and talk and discuss). I was beginning to feel a little nauseous, and I asked them, in conclusion, if they would agree to allow our nurse to show them how to use a condom, and heads nodded in agreement. I knew I would not get an agreement to stop FGM as decisions like this would have to be given over to a full meeting of all tribal leaders, but I had hoped that

I had made an in-way for further discussion. FGM is the drum that I beat whenever I am with the Maasai. I have too many children in our care that had come under the razor blade.

The next day, whilst the volunteers along with one of LIA cooks started to teach the Maasai mama's about hygiene prior to preparing the food, we had a special menu that we prepared each time to try to introduce proteins into the diet of the Maasai's. First on the menu was going to be fish soup with bread, followed by chicken stew with rice and then local fruits. I had as always been assured that the Maasai would not eat the fish soup as they considered fish to be like a snake, and refused to eat it. But as I had won over other Maasai villages to change their diets so their children would not succumb and die from Kwashiorkor or Marasma which is a lack of protein in their diets, I knew I had to keep trying. I went over to see how the preparations were progressing, as our driver was starting to light the fires between the three stones which would hold the large cooking pots that could feed 100 people from each pot.

The volunteers were working with a group of young, Maasai girls and older women and were now pealing the onions, potatoes and carrots. One group was cleaning the fish, and the Maasai mama was reluctant to hold one, preferring to look not to touch. I then saw our nurse going into the school room talking with some oversea visitors who had just arrived, and she was carrying her familiar bag of 'goodies' which held such things as condoms to give out and plastic and wooden phallic symbols which would help her demonstrate how to 'put on a condom'. One of the names that I had acquired as I tried to stem the spread of the HIV/AIDS virus by dishing out thousands of condoms each year was 'mama condom'.

Small groups were filtering into the classroom. On this occasion, I decided I was going to keep away so the interpreter wouldn't have to change the language from Kiswahili into English.

Over 200 children and mama's were present for the meal, and the routine was always the same. The youngest children would lead the long line for the first course carrying a plate or dish in their hands with a spoon followed by the elderly mama's, then the teenage girls, and lastly the married mama's. They would then return again to the line with their plates for the chicken stew, fruits, and drink. I have this very clear memory of standing and watching seven Maasai men surrounded by a field of sitting children and women eating the fish soup. These seven leaders kept looking around and pointing with their sticks, scratching their bald heads as something never before seen was being witnessed.

At the end of the meal I asked the crowd of women if they had enjoyed the meal, and a hand clap followed. "Did you like the fish soup?" I asked tentatively, and nods of approval followed. "But if you liked the fish soup why don't you eat it? It is very cheap to eat and is full of goodness for you and your children." I was stunned by the reply. "Because no one has shown us how to cook it."

We arrived back at Mailisita, our rented 15 room home near to Moshi, tired and wanting a nice long shower (not with just a limited amount of water from a bucket), and a hearty meal. According to the volunteers, basic living was OK for a short period of time but not something that they would like to endure on a regular basis.

Some months later, whilst working in the office with Coupa, I received a phone call from a young lady in Kenya who had been present when our nurse had been giving the seminar on HIV/AIDS and how to use the condom to stop the virus spread and reduce pregnancies.

She told me this story… After LIA left Kenya, she decided that she would also hold a seminar on the prevention of the spread of the virus with another village group of Maasai men in a different area, but she did not have a phallic symbol to use like we had to demonstrate the art of placing on a condom, so she decided to use a banana. She was just ringing me to tell me that she had been stopped along the road by a very irate Maasai moran(which could have led to serious repercussions), who complained bitterly to her that she had told him - and all his friends heard her say this - that, if he used a condom, his wife would not have a baby, and now his wife has told him she is having another child, and IT WAS all her fault for lying to him. "But what did you do," she asked, "for your wife to get pregnant?" "Well," he said, "I went to the market and bought a banana, and at night, I put the condom on the banana and put it on the chair at the side of my bed, and then I had sex with my wife. Now she's pregnant, and it's all your fault!" The young lady on the end of the phone was very serious as she relayed the Maasai's anger at what had happened.

I tried very hard to empathize and to keep her from hearing my barely controlled laughter. When I switched the phone off, I very un-kindly laughed and laughed until I wept tears at the scene the young lady had so vividly painted for me over the phone. I re-told the story to Coupa who also burst out laughing, and that started me laughing again. We were still chuckling when our nurse arrived into the office. She asked me what we were laughing at so heartily about, and I quick-ly said, "You'll never believe what happened after you gave that sem-inar in Kenya to the Maasai." I gleefully described the events that I had just been told. But whilst Coupa and I were still in fits of laughter again, the nurse kept a straight face. Coupa and I exchanged glances. Surely it was at least worth a smile or a grimace, but no, apparently not! She looked off into the distance as if miles away, and thoughtfully said, "Well I suppose when I go up the mountain I will now have to remember to take the phallics with me after this, because when I have done some impromptu seminars, I've always used a cucumber!...."

Such is the price paid for education!

CHAPTER EIGHTEEN
FROZEN AWARENESS

(Readers with a sensitive disposition should not read this true story).

ne day, the watchman came to my office door and informed me there was a young lady visitor to see me. "Sit her on the bench please whilst I complete these reports and then I will come over and see her." I looked up as a young girl passed by my window. She looked to be about eighteen or nineteen years of age, and she was very attractive.

After closing the file I had been working on, I went out to speak with the young girl. She had her arm covered with a kanga (a piece of material) and my first thought from seeing the way that she was holding her arm it could possibly be broken.

After the customary greeting of "shikamoo mama" and my response of "marahaba," she undid the kanga which was tied around her neck and let the material fall to her waist. I took a step back in shock. I was expecting a broken wrist or a cut. I was not expecting to see the whole of the girls arm burnt black. I called for an interpreter to find out how this accident had happened. I was told that the young lady suffered from epileptic fits and had fallen into the fire and that was how her arm had become burnt. The local traditional midwife had suggested that she should come to see me to see if I could offer her any assistance.

I made arrangements immediately to escort Susan (not her real name) to the local hospital, and she was immediately admitted. The hospital doctor removed all the burnt skin from her wrist to the top of her arm leaving just a pink arm. I gave her some money to purchase some food, paid an advance on the medical bill, and returned home to the center.

Two days later, I went to visit Susan at the hospital to find out when she would be discharged.

As I passed the ward sister's station, she saw me and came out of her office, greeting me, and pulling me to one side. "We have a problem," she said, and looked both ways to see if anyone was listening to our conversation. " We have managed to reduce the seizures that the girl was having by prescribing a drug, but she is disturbing all the other patients by howling like an animal at night, and it really is upsetting everyone. Can you take her home with you once the doctor has discharged her?" "Well yes. I can do that," I agreed, feeling a little bewildered. Was she being discharged because her condition had improved or because she was disturbing the other patients? How strange. I tried to comprehend why someone would howl like an animal in the night. Perhaps it was a re-occurring nightmare or something.

I collected Susan from the ward, purchased the drugs from the hospital dispensary, and caught the public transport back to the center.

I asked our local village leader to make sure that Susan always took her medicine each day to control the amount of seizures and before the packet was empty, if she let me know, I would purchase Susan some more drugs. I also mentioned what the Ward Sister had said to me about keeping everyone awake at night with her howling like an animal. "That's not as surprising as you might think, because she lives with her grandparents, and they are both traditional witchdoctors. They have probably bewitched her!" After this surprising conversation which I was of course hesitant to believe, the community leader returned to say that the grandparents had thrown the drugs into the fire and refused to allow their granddaughter to take them saying that they would be treating her themselves.

I asked LIA's midwife to go and counsel the grandparents as she came from the same village as Susan. She returned saying that mountain people found it hard to make changes in their lives as they believed in different spirits and not this new medicine.

About a year later, the community leader came to the center to find me. She said that Susan was in a terrible state. She had helped Susan deliver a baby girl, and she was having uncontrollable seizures one after the other. "Please hurry and come and see her." When I arrived at the house, Susan was on the floor jerking and eye's rolling. We picked her up, the driver lifting her top torso and me carrying her legs and we placed her in the vehicle and drove immediately to the local dispensary to get her stabilized. After settling her in, we returned to collect the baby girl and take her into our nursery, because, obviously, Susan was in no fit state to care for her new-born baby.

Once again, I paid the medical bill and wanted Susan to return to the center with me to enable her to bond with her new baby, but she refused, saying she wanted to stay on the mountain. This time Light in Africa's doctor went to counsel the grandparents. He returned saying they agreed whilst he was with them, but he thought that they would throw the drugs away again after he had left their house.

We had bought a near 'scrapper' of a pick-up truck to continue the work that we were involved with on the mountain, and my daughter returned with a volunteer to the center looking mordantly pale. "Are you alright?" I asked. "You look sick! Do you need to get a malaria test?" She supported herself on the bonnet of the truck, and said "I have Susan in the back of the truck. She smells terrible, and I think that she has gangrene." I walked to the back of the truck and climbed up on the tail bar to look in the back of the truck. Susan was lying on a dirty piece of mattress with flies buzzing over her extensively burnt leg, where this time the fire had burnt her so badly it had welded her toes together. Trying to control the vomit that was making its way up from my stomach, I jumped down from the back of the truck. "What happened?" I asked my daughter.

She told me the following story: I was close to Susan's house and just thought I would call and tell her how her baby was thriving, when a neighbor arrived and said that Susan was locked in a room, and she hadn't seen her for over two weeks. I sent a 'runner' to go find the grandparents who were working in the fields. When they arrived, I demanded that they open the door, and they did so very reluctantly. "That's when I found her, mum. When the door opened, the smell was horrendous, she had lain there for two weeks without as much as an aspirin." My daughter was very close to collapsing, so I suggested that she and the volunteer go and take a 'hot' shower and get some food down them and I would take Susan straight to hospital.

Going into my room and grabbing my handbag, I returned to the truck and started the engine. I drove straight to casualty, found a stretcher, and with the help of a nurse, pushed her into a cubicle for the casualty doctor to take a look at her. He was shocked at her condition to say the least, and his voice rose in anguish as he started to question me as to how 'this girl' had gotten into this condition. "Don't shout at me," I retaliated. "My daughter has just found her. She has been locked in a room for two weeks with not so much as one pain relief pill." He picked up a kidney dish, and with a pair of tweezers, started to pull the maggots out from her ankle bone one by one and drop them into the kidney dish. "This is terrible," the doctor said in a lower tone of voice. "She may have to have her leg amputated." I watched silently as he extracted another maggot from the wound. "There's too many in here. I might miss some. Nurse, hand me the iodine please." He poured a capful of iodine straight in to the wound, where you could clearly see her ankle bone. Susan didn't even flinch; she just continued to wrap a piece of material around and around her hand. "What now?" I asked the doctor. "She needs to be admitted," he responded. "Are you going to pay the hospital bill?" I nodded.

As the lift was "out of action," the auxiliary nurse and I had to push the stretcher up three flights to the ward that Susan would be admitted to. I waited in the corridor for three hours standing in front of Susan's leg so that passersby would not bump into it. "That's it," I thought. "I've had enough," and walked over to the nursing station. "Doctor," I said. "I have a patient here who has possible gangrene and might have to have her leg amputated. Can you tell me please if you have any bed space on the ward?" "No," he responded. "Corridor space only." "Well I am going to make your job easier by removing this patient from this ward and taking her to a private hospital. All that I need from you is the diagnoses and the treatment plan, and I will get out of your hair." He left the station and went to look at the leg and winced. He went and brought another doctor for a second opinion, and they gave me a paper listing the medical requirements. I phoned our Light in Africa doctor, and although it was late, asked him to meet me at the private hospital, to which he agreed. I asked for an orderly to help me with the stretcher, but no one had arrived after thirty minutes, so I pushed the trolley by myself out of the ward while carefully navigating it. In the corridor, I saw a man enjoying a puff on a cigarette and asked him to help me for $2.00, to which he readily agreed.

LIA's doctor was waiting for me at the private hospital. It was now nearly 11pm, and I was deeply grateful for our doctor's commitment to our children. We had worked together on many cases, and he always stayed with me until everything was sorted out. On one occasion, a child had died in the middle of the night and we had to visit three mortuaries until we found one with space to take the child. You quickly begin to have a lot of respect for doctors like this.

The doctor quickly arranged for the night security to fetch a wheel chair, and Susan was transferred into it and carried up to a two bedded room. He also arranged for the second bed to be made up for me, bless him, and I quickly fell asleep. The next morning, as I awoke, the hospital doctor was looking intensely at Susan's leg, and the mobile X-ray machine arrived. The mature radiologist set to work in placing Susan's leg in exactly the right position for the plate to take a good picture. "Have you noticed anything about this patient?" he said, and not knowing where the question was going to lead I shook my head.

"She hasn't made a moan or a groan at all, and she is staring at the wall whilst I move her burnt leg about." The penny dropped! "Yes,your right," I responded. I now recalled from my time as a social worker that this was called "Frozen Awareness." It usually meant that the mind had undergone such trauma that it had just 'switched off.'

Each day, the doctor would lather her burnt leg with pure honey, and after three weeks in hospital the doctor said that she could come and stay at the home with us, and Light in Africa's doctor could continue the treatment at our facility. For me, I thought it was a good idea for the mother of the baby that we had cared for, who was now 'toddling' about, to get to know each other and hopefully some bonding would take place.

Susan was now doing well, and she could place her foot on the floor and 'hobble' around and get herself to the toilet. Her daughter was brought to her on many occasions, but it could have been any child as there just was no maternal instinct at all towards the child. Susan had now gained weight and her gaunt features were disappearing to be replaced by the attractive women that I had first met.

Her family visited her, and Susan said she wanted to go back home with them. "No way!" I exclaimed. "She can't do that! She is living independent of her witchdoctor family, and she hasn't 'howled' in month's now. Prayers have sorted that problem out." Two weeks followed of long drawn out discussions with the social worker, the medical team, and the family. I was totally against her going back to the family and couldn't express myself sufficiently of the dangers that Susan would face going back. At least with us, she was alive and well, and on it went, more meetings, more dialogue. The midwife pointed out to me that Susan was over twenty one years of age, so she was not a minor anymore, and they could ask the village leader to go in and monitor the situation. At this comment, I rounded on the midwife, "Oh yes, and haven't we heard all this before?" I replied angrily. "Don't you think it is all rather strange that it is always the fire that she falls into. Never the river, or a fall down the mountain into the valley.

It's always the fire. I asked Susan once again, "Do you really want to go back home and leave your little girl with us?" "Yes," she replied. "In that case, I am going to be like Pontus Pilate. I'm going to wash my hands of this whole affair. This is so terribly wrong. She is going to put herself in mortal danger again." And with that comment I left the room.

Sometime later, Susan allegedly fell into the fire and was burnt to death.

After the funeral, the family came to the center to take their granddaughter, and my comment to them was, "Over my dead body."

CHAPTER NINETEEN
BEAUTY IN A T-SHIRT

It was going to be another scorching hot day as I caught the local dala dala from the mountain bus stand to go to my final destination at Moshi to purchase stores for the center. The limited amount of road safety precautions that surround these public vehicles means that these mini buses which should hold a maximum of 15 passengers can operate with as many as 30 passengers who are squeezed in like sardines in a tin of oil. Often the sliding door will drop off, and the vehicle has to stop to change the tyres due to the canvas thread being easily seen, but as I did not have any vehicle of my own and had to walk everywhere or use this very unsafe local transport, my options were limited.

As there were only a few passengers getting on at the first stop, I was able to choose my seat. Gaining a few inches of space now was vastly important so that when it started to get full and overflowing with people standing and leaning over you, one could treasure this couple of inches of extra space. The journey began, and the dala dala soon began to fill-up. I was sat at the front by a window seat so I was able to watch passengers, armed with sacks of rice and maize, live chickens or even a goat, and fruits and vegetables, get on and off the dala. It is not uncommon to see a mother with a young child get on and place the child on the nearest passenger's knee, male or female, whilst she carried her bags to another seat that was available. Something like that would never happen in Europe, with all the child protection issues, and the child would sit on a complete strangers lap until the mother was ready to leave, possibly to try to sell a few items at the market to enable her to feed her family. The dala stopped, and I saw this pretty young teenager trying to run to catch the dala. What struck me most was that I had never seen an African lady wearing high stiletto heels before. This was something very new. She managed to climb up the steps and squeeze into a front seat facing the other passengers. Everyone stared at her. Comments were made by some mama's who rigidly stuck to the usual long kanga dresses, and considered this young girl 'most inappropriately' dressed in a way that violated the African dress code. But in my opinion, this 17-18year old girl looked stunning. She had worked really hard at looking like a European tourist. I noted her newly-braided extension, brown wool hair, and her red painted finger and toe nails that peaked out of her open front high heeled shoes. She was very much appreciating being admired by the bus conductor as she kept flicking her long brown plaited braids back off her face, the T shirt she was wearing was spotlessly white, and she sported a pretty necklace.

Her skin tight jeans were also something the new generation was now into, and you could purchase these denim jeans second-hand, very cheaply from the local market. I mulled over the changes that were now taking place in Tanzania. I remembered when I first arrived in the area in 1999, all the houses appeared to be painted cream and blue and that was it. Now a change was definitely taking place as traditional ideas were dying out, and a new generation of independent spirit was emerging, and houses were now being painted in many different colours from purple (that the Asian community particularly favoured) to lime green. And with the access of mobile phones and computers, this under-developed country was moving forward in leaps and bounds. The thousands of tourists who visit the area each year to either climb Mount Kilimanjaro or to visit the National Parks were helping to make this change possible as they brought with them

into the country, new technology from iPods to interactive play stations that all the youth wanted to acquire and own.

A few kilometers down the road, the dala dala came to a halt and
the young lady gingerly got up from the seat to get off at this stop. She
steadied herself by holding on to a passenger's shoulder, she slowly negotiated the steps, and started to walk away. The driver put the vehicle
into first gear, and as we slowly pulled away from the side of the road,
I was able to get a rear view of the young lady trying to walk ever so
sedately in her obviously new stiletto shoes. I looked up and read the
message on the back of her T shirt. It read 'Mortuary Attendant!' The
image was shattered!

CHAPTER TWENTY

LIFESAVING

I was having a fight with the wind as I tried to peg out some washing on the clothes line, and a white sheet insisted in wrapping itself around me, when everyone in the courtyard turned towards the gate. We heard the 'Chagga' tribes scream for help. This scream sounds like the word "whooeee whooeee," which informs neighbors or anyone close by that someone needs help and is in imminent danger. Security had unlocked the gate and stepped outside to see where the noise was coming from, when suddenly a women ran straight through the gate, stopped and looked around at her surroundings. She spotted me with a mouthful of pegs in my mouth, ran over to me, and placed a screaming wet baby into my arms. She was quickly followed through the gate by another women who was screaming abuse at her and was clearly very angry.

I turned my back to protect the baby from any blows that might occur and called for a kitchen staff member to come and take the baby from me and take it into the kitchen.

Security and staff members were now running to try to separate the enraged woman from the other woman. Her eyes were full of anger as she continued to scream and berate the woman who had given me the baby. When, eventually, some semblance of order was maintained, we all listened to the first woman who had rushed into the center. She told us the story that she was on her way to purchase some vegetables for the evening meal. When she reached the river to cross over on the stones, she saw the second woman trying to drown the baby in the water. She had waded into the water and snatched the baby from the mother, and all that she could think to do was run with the baby to Light in Africa's children's home.

This was a pretty serious case, and obviously this women had some major problems. We sat them both down and offered a cup of tea and some bread, and after hearing all of the facts, I said we would take care of the baby until the social welfare department could make an investigation of the case.

We found out that the baby's mother suffered from Epilepsy, had a mental problem, and she already had five children. All of the requirements were completed, and we were asked if we would keep the little baby girl. At the request of the family, our midwife offered the mother the contraceptive device and this was fitted in to her arm.

A year later, our store manager was busy purchasing the weekly fruit and vegetables from the local market, when she heard a commotion coming from a near-by tree and joined a large crowd that was gathering. A baby boy had been abandoned underneath the tree, and local leaders were trying to find out from anyone if they had seen a mother with the baby. A store holder remembered seeing the mother with the baby, and she gave a clue to who the mother might be. Our store manager came to the conclusion that it could possibly be the same mother who had tried to drown the baby girl. Along with the fruits and vegetables, she also brought the baby boy back to the center with her.

Our midwife visited the mother to find out why the contraceptive had not worked only to find that the mother had removed the device, hence another child.

The Executive Committee of LIA was involved in the usual Monday morning meeting to discuss everything that had happened during the previous week and make a plan of action for the coming week.

I was sat back in a chair enjoying a cup of tea, in order that the conversation between the staff could be carried out in their mother tongue of Kiswahili, instead of having to stop to interpret for me into English. As I sat there, I started to feel a sense of fear. And then fear for a baby. I placed my cup down on the coffee table and sat still. I waited quietly until I received clearer understanding of what the 'sense' meant. I interrupted the meeting by asking a staff manager to get in the vehicle and go immediately to the home of the mother of whom we have two of her children in care. "But why?" he asked. "I have to be totally honest, I have no idea. I can't really place everything together except to say there is a baby in "extreme danger." Please humor me, get in the car, and go see how the mother is, and take a carer with you." Eyebrows were raised as he looked at the other committee members, and he left the room.

Some hours later, the vehicle returned, and I was most anxious to find out if that 'sense' had proven positive or futile. It indeed was proven to be a correct feeling when the carer walked through the door holding a baby girl. And the story was told. The mother had given birth to another baby and had taken the child into a field full of tall maize along with a knife to dispose of the baby.

Thank God, a family member became suspicious of her actions, followed her into the field, and had stopped her from inflicting wounds to the child. Light in Africa's vehicle arrived just as the two women immerged from the field. The baby girl was brought straight into our family to join her other sister and brother.

The mother died shortly after this event took place during a seizure.

CHAPTER TWENTY-ONE
NO MONEY IN THE BANK NO MONEY IN MY PURSE

ach Monday morning, I would travel to Moshi, our nearest town, to purchase food supplies. First, I would go to the bank and withdraw sufficient funds to purchase the goods and have enough to give to the kitchen staff each day. I asked the cashier for a balance and found that all the money that I had placed into the account three years earlier from the UK had practically dwindled away. I withdrew sufficient money to purchase the stores and left just enough in the account to keep it open, and sent up an arrow prayer for God to touch some kind persons heart to make a donation into our account.

Next door to the bank was a restaurant where I could enjoy a pot of tea very cheaply and this was my Monday morning 'treat'. Whilst waiting for the tea to arrive, I looked at my store list once again. I must purchase the formula milk for the new baby, but the 'toddler's and the older children were all now drinking cow's milk. I thought, "How can I reduce the list? My money has lasted me nearly three years, and it hasn't just been used for the thirty two children and staff at the center but also to help hundreds of people on the mountain and saved lives, but what am I going to do for next week's money? All I can ever do is pray; I will have to go into 'fasting' mode for next week's finances."

I returned home to the center and the goods were distributed into the store, and the following day a neighbor's child was brought to me who had been badly burnt when the child had fallen into a fire. I used the daily money that I should give to the kitchen staff to pay for the hospital treatment for the child. Now I had no money in my purse and no money in the bank. I did not mention the financial situation to anyone, and all day long I was sending up 'arrow prayers' for finances to come into the center. That night I couldn't sleep for worrying about the situation. How was I going to tell mama Coupa in the morning that she had no money for the daily food items?

At 3:00 a.m., I put on my dressing gown and decided to have a look in the store room to see if I could use any fruits or vegetables to make a meal. As I shone my torch around the store, all that I could see in the dim light was ten carrots. My singular pity party started to go into first gear as I knelt on the floor and asked for an audience in the throne room of heaven. "Dear God. This is just so unfair. I have left everything for the gospel; my family, my friends, my little luxury lifestyle. I willingly left it all behind for You. But how can I face the kitchen staff today with no money? This is just so unfair! Let's get this right, Lord. You're the miracle worker, and I'm the servant. I can't do anything without you. Please help me."

At around 5:00 a.m., I got up from my knees and went into my room to take a shower. No good putting the inevitable off any longer. I have to face the music. At 6:30 a.m., I opened the door to go to the kitchen and enjoy my usual morning cup of tea. The wind was blowing my long skirt around my ankles as I started walking along the path. "Zawadi, zawadi," (gift gift) I hear a male voice shout. I look up to where the voice is coming from, and there is a hand hanging over our 10' high gate. In the hand is a note waving about in the breeze. My first thought was , "Quick. Go grab that money before it blows away." I bolted down the path, took a run and a jump, and grabbed the money out of the man's hand, uttering "Mungu Akurbiriki" (God Bless You). I held the note very tightly close to my chest, and I started to walk down the path. The enormity of the situation hit me, and I turned around to look at the gate. How on earth can someone have a hand hanging over a 10' high gate? It was impossible, unless they were standing on someone's shoulders or on a step ladder. I turned around and proceeded to the kitchen. I nonchalantly placed the note, like I did every morning, under the salt pot and was handed my cup of tea which I drank, and then went back to my room to pray and ask for forgiveness for all the awful things that I had said earlier on in the morning. In the afternoon, a father of one of the babies whose wife had died in childbirth brought a stalk of green bananas. I counted them all. There were 76 green bananas, and I lugged and pulled the heavy stalk into the kitchen, asking the staff to make a banana stew for dinner that evening and use the ten carrots that were in the store (This is a traditional Tanzanian dish).

That evening, I did my rounds as usual, going into the nursery first. All the babies and toddlers were fast asleep under their mosquito nets and all were washed, well-fed, and 'shiny'. I then went into the dormitory where the night nurse was folding the days washing and all the children were 'sound asleep'. I returned to my bedroom, knelt down, and said, "Dear God, I still have no money in the bank and no money in my purse, but today you have proved to me what a Providing God you are for all of our needs. Today, I make you this promise. If my life has to have any meaning to the people that visit with us, they must see the Hand of God at work in this mission. From today, I will never again ask for any funding or any materials. It will all be done by prayer only. Because You are the one who touches the hearts and minds of the people to give without counting the cost, and not to seek for any reward. This is my promise to you tonight."

Over these thirteen years, there has never been one day when the children in our care have not received three full square meals per day. On any given midweek day, we are preparing over 1,000 meals, which includes the food kitchen that we operate to feed all the vulnerable children at the mining town. It is all done through prayer. I personally only receive 3,200 pound sterling a year from my work and government pension, and I think the UK poverty line is around 15,000 pound sterling. As a volunteer with LIA, all that is provided for me is a bed to sleep on and food to eat. I have no permanent accommodation, and I can be sleeping in a tent or in a room whatever happens to be available. In one year, I moved fourteen times. A pilgrim, it is said, is always on the move, and I can vouch for that. I have learnt to live without any materialism in my life, and it is quite a relief. Whereby once I loved to collect bone china tea services, and I slept in a bed over 100 years old, my collector's items now are the lives of as many children as I can save, and I try to ensure they all have a sound education and a chance of a happy, successful life.

This poem, Taking Up My Position, was written by an African Pastor who was martyred, and it describes eloquently just how I feel.

I am part of the Fellowship of the unashamed. I have the Holy Spirit power. The die has been cast. I've stepped over the line. The decision has been made. I am a disciple of His. I won't look back, let up, slow down, or be still. My past is redeemed, my present makes sense, and my future is secure.

I am finished with low living, sight walking, small-planning, smooth knees, colorless dreams, tame vision, mundane talking, miserly giving, or dwarfed goals.

I no longer need pre-eminence, prosperity, position, promotions, plaudits or popularity. I don't have to be right, first, top, recognized, praised, regarded, or rewarded. I now live by presence, learn by faith, love by patience, lift by prayer, and labor by power.

My face is set, my gait is fast, my goal is heaven, my road is narrow, my way is rough, my companions few, my guide reliable, my mission clear. I cannot be bought, compromised, detoured, lured away, turned back, diluted, or delayed. I will not flinch in the face of sacrifice, hesitate in the presence of adversity, negotiate at the table of the enemy, ponder at the pool of popularity, or meander in the maze of mediocrity.

I won't give up, shut up, let up, or burn up till I've preached up, prayed up, paid up, stored up, and stayed the course of Christ.

I am a disciple of Jesus, I must go till He comes, give till I drop, preach till all know, and work till He stops.

And when He comes to get His own, He'll have no problems recognizing me. My colors will be clear.

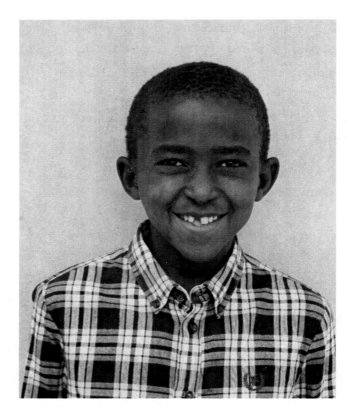

Before   After

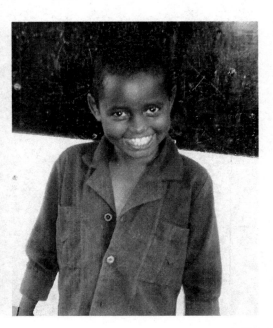

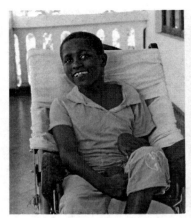

CHAPTER TWENTY-TWO
THE ATTACK

Another beautiful day on Mount Kilimanjaro. How I loved the natural beauty that surrounded the children's home. The banana and coffee trees growing on the plantations and the blossoming bougainvillea with its variety of stunning colors just gladdened one's heart. The air felt fresh after the early morning downpour as I pushed a pair of trousers to the bottom of my back pack just in case I fell on the slippery slope. I could really have done without the extra weight, but needs must, I thought. I finished my cup of tea, and Mama Coupa helped me on with my large backpack and pushed spare plastic bags inside the open zip pocket, just in case I needed extra bags for the vegetables. She then handed me the list of food supplies that I needed to purchase after I had been to the bank.

Joanne, our first volunteer from Canada, was busy playing with the little children on the grass, and as I passed, she asked all the little ones to give me a wave and blow me a kiss, which I had to stop and throw kisses and more kisses to them as they learnt this new skill. One little one was blowing raspberries, and Joanne took hold of her hand, started to lift it to her mouth, and repeated, "blow a kiss to mama, blow a kiss to mama." It was sheer joy to see them happy and smiling.

I stepped outside the gates, and I could hear the padlock being fitted after my departure. I started to carefully negotiate the steep downward path, grabbing hold of any greenery that I could make a grab for to enable me to stay upright.

The dala dala (public transport) was waiting for passengers, and I was the first to enter and take a seat. It was to be a further fifty minutes before the next two passengers arrived. I asked the conductor 'When are we leaving?" and he casually replied, "When we're full." "But this could take hours before your full," I said. "Sijui," (I don't know) and he shrugged his shoulders and moved on. After a further forty minutes delay, the vehicle started to move down the mountain picking up passengers as we went. It stopped outside a dispensary for a heavily pregnant woman to alight and slowly try to navigate past the standing passengers. A lady kindly arose from her seat and motioned for her to sit down in the seat in front of me. Already there was a goat under her seat which had been pushed under earlier creating very little leg room for me. "No wonder," I thought, "tourists bought T shirts which read' "I survived a dala dala ride." Once again, I bemoaned to God as to why I didn't have a vehicle, and that it would just make my life so much easier. But I had already received my answer to that question, and that was whilst I am walking, I am talking and greeting people, and they all know I am on the mountain doing God's work because God brought me to the mountain all the way from the UK. If I had a vehicle, I would just zip past in a world of my own, instead of walking every day experiencing the African ways, African culture, and African needs.

The goat started to lick at some fluid which was wetting my boot and trickling along the groves of the metal floor of the dala dala.

"Dear God! The woman's waters have broken!" I thought. I opened a side pocket of the back pack and handed the lady some tissues and a plastic bag. She was obviously on her way to Moshi hospital to have her baby delivered. She smiled wanly at me as she took the items from me.

I just managed to squeeze into the bank as they were closing the doors for the day.

Because of the long delay with the transport, I had to miss my usual two cups of tea at my oasis, and rushed around from shop to shop purchasing the stores. It was 6:30 p.m. before the dala dala departed from Moshi. This was not good. The rules for the family and volunteers was to always make sure to be back in the centre before darkness fell each evening at 7:00 p.m. As we lived only a couple of hundred kilometers from the equator, we have very little variance from dawn to dusk so usually it is quite easy to calculate what time it is, and now due to the lateness of the transport, I would have to climb the mountain in the dark.

I crossed the road at Kwasadala market to catch another dala dala which would take me the ten kilometers up the mountain to the bus stop.

There was already a scramble and a push for the few remaining seats, and I managed to get the last seat before I would have had to stand precariously holding onto anything that was available in the form of support. As we waited for even more passengers to be herded inside, something started to stir in my spirit. I started to feel that something was terribly wrong. "What is it? Whatever am I feeling?" I questioned myself. "How strange."

The vehicle started moving, and I started to shuffle around in my seat. I felt consumed with a sense of real fear and danger I wondered if something was going to happen to this dala dala. I started to silently pray for the protection of the vehicle and the passengers and driver. When I stopped praying, this sense of danger and foreboding became even more intense. What can I do? I prayed again asking for clearer understanding as to what these emotions meant. As I waited for the journey to reach its stop, I felt a real resigning sense of doom that something was going to happen to me. I made a decision. If any other passenger leaves the dala dala at my stop I'm going to ask them if I can walk up the mountain to the center with them. "Please God, let someone get off at my stop. I don't want to walk up the steep mountain by myself. It doesn't feel safe. I don't know if all this anxiety is because I'm on the mountain in the dark, but please protect me on this journey home."

Two men pushed their way past the standing passengers followed by me. And as the dala disappeared, I asked the two men if I could walk up the mountain with them. This action alone could have placed me in a vulnerable position, but I felt that I had no other choice. The men agreed to my request, and we started to walk the only road that led to the home. We crossed the river which irrigates the coffee trees and started the steep climb. Houses were becoming sparser, and as we past the last house with a fluorescent light outside the gate, the only thing that I can recall from memory is seeing two tall ladies dressed in full traditional African clothes, including material wrapped around the head to make a hat, and thinking that they must be all dressed up to go to a party.

As we continued to climb, the taller man of the two, kept turning around and saying to me, "Pastor Malcolm, mbaya sana, mbaya sana (very bad) (very bad)" and he clenched his wrists together which in sign language represented handcuffs. The man took my hand, placed me in between the two men, and pushed on my back to try to make me hurry up. Three times during this exhausting journey to the top, did this man turn around and repeat the same words. And I totally failed to understand the significance of his actions. As all three of us reached the top and stood on firm ground, with our arms akimbo, perspiration pouring from me with carrying the heavy backpack, we gasped for breath. The tall man pushed me once again to start walking to the center which was close by. As I started to walk, still panting for breath, I turned, and I could see his shadow from the light of the moon, standing there watching me to make sure I arrived home safely.

The following morning I had a visitor. It was the tall man who had helped me home safely the night before. He needed to tell me something. My interpreter listened to the story intently and became grave, as he repeated the man's sentences word for word.

The tall man had returned back down the mountain to confront the two women who had been following us. He had recognized who they were, Pastor Malcolm and his nephew. "Why did you stop us from killing the wazungu," the pastor had demanded. "We have a pit dug and a truck waiting to cut her up in little bits and dispose of her body, and you stopped us." The enormity of the situation hit me.

The intense feeling of awareness the Holy Spirit had given me was for me to act upon it, and only by walking with these two men had my life been saved. I then realized that if I had climbed the mountain alone, I most certainly would have been killed, and my family would never have known what had happened to me.

I asked the tall man if he would accompany me to the local police station and make a statement to that effect, and he said he would.

Three weeks after this event, the tall man came to see me early on a Sunday morning. As he stood in front of me, he burst into tears. I was embarrassed to see this big African man resolved to tears and didn't quite know what to do. I left the room to make him a cup of tea and fetch an interpreter. After he had composed himself, he told this story. Pastor Malcolm had visited his home one night and said, "If you don't continue to stand with the wazungu in a court case I will give you money," and the tall man had replied, "I'll think about it." Again Pastor Malcolm had visited the tall man's home and this time he had told him, "If you continue to stand with the wazungu, against your own people, watch out that your calf isn't poisoned," and he had left. Then three nights ago, he had visited his home and said, "Don't sleep, I'm going to burn your house down with you, your wife, and kids in it." So for three nights, the tall man had patrolled his home making sure his family were safe, and working in his field the next day. This morning, he had found his calf dead. It had been poisoned, and he broke down once again in to tears shaking his head, saying, "I can't stand with you anymore. This man is evil."

I asked the tall man how much his calf would have cost to purchase it from the market, and he gave me the price. I went into my room and removed sufficient money from my wallet to purchase the man another calf. Whilst in my room, I prayed to God for understanding, grace, and wisdom to handle this situation which was all now way above my head. I returned to the office asked the interpreter to make sure the man understood that I would now act and stop this man from harming his family. He should now go home and try to get some sleep.

One of the statements that people sometimes make about the British public, is that you can push them, and push them, and push them until their backs are up against a wall, and then you had better watch out.

And that was the position that I found myself in. I had been pushed and had accepted all kinds of allegations of abuse that I had supposedly had committed, but I had done nothing in return. I had turned the other cheek. (Mathew 5-39) I had had a threat of poisoning against me, and I had to stop attending the out-reach dispensaries which I loved to do, and had a shotgun fired over my head, yet nothing had been done to protect me, my family, the children, or anyone in the center.

Now with the tall man in such desperate despair, I had to make a move to protect everyone in the center and this man's family.

The following day, I journeyed to Moshi and headed for my friendly travel agents office. I explained to him the events what had happened. He sat me down in front of a computer and said, "Type a letter to the British Embassy in Dar es Salaam explaining all the events that have happened to you, and I will fax it over to them."

The following day, a police Land Rover packed full of officers with guns along with their Commanding Officer arrived at the center. After I had recalled all the events that had happened, he said, "How on earth you have survived living on this mountain for three years, I just don't know."

"Will you leave the mountain now?" he asked. "Only when God tells me to," I replied, "not before."

I had to visit the police station four days later to make a statement. The detective in the room started to chuckle as I was writing the statement, and I looked up questioningly. "When we arrived at the Pastors house to arrest him," the detective said, "I asked him to put his hands out so that I could place the handcuffs on him, and he said, 'You can't arrest me I'm a Pastor!' and I replied, 'Ahhh, don't worry about that. Two weeks ago I arrested a Bishop." This statement was the only slightly amusing incident in the whole tragic saga.

My lawyer informed me that the case was 'too sensitive' to take to court, and the 'Imposter of a Pastor' was released from custody three days later. Thankfully, he never bothered me or anyone else again.

Always.
A Christian's life
is a life of daring
rich in risks.
yet a rich life.
A dangerous path
because
it's a path of love.
And whoever
gets away
on this path
without wounds
without damage
must ask himself
whether he is on the right path.
Jesus Christ
and with Him all
who follow Him
will be recognized
by their readiness
to get wounded.

CHAPTER TWENTY-THREE
BETRAYAL

There was much excitement in the center as the kitchen staff boiled a saucepan full of eggs, buttered huge amounts of bread, washed the fruit, and filled the flasks with tea, as preparations were made to harvest our maize which would give sufficient sacks of flour to feed the children for the following year.

Harry was the plantation manager of the local coffee farm, and he had kindly allowed us to plant some acreage of maize which was well irrigated. On inspection the staff came back and reported a 'bumper' crop to harvest. Members of staff, my family, and the older children left in a pick-up truck to harvest the crop, and Pastor Alfred said he thought it would be a good idea that, after the maize had been gathered, the hired truck could take it all to his home, and he would have his older boys beat it off the stalks and then bag it up ready for milling. I thanked him for his generous gesture as I thought the process if it were to be performed in the center might make quite a mess. The group returned exhausted but happy that the mission had been successfully accomplished, and it was indeed a high yield of maize that had been delivered. We gave God the Glory that He had provided sufficient flour to feed our children.

Strangely enough, Pastor Alfred who had been a very regular visitor to our center each week for over three years, had not been seen for more than a month.

On impulse, I hired a pick-up truck, put the older boys in the back, and went to collect our sacks of maize from the Pastor's house.

On arrival, we were met by his wife who quite openly informed me that Pastor Alfred had sold the maize and spent the money. The flour for the year was all gone. I have not seen or heard from Pastor Alfred from that day forward.

Betrayal of trust is such a bitter pill to swallow, and forgiveness is the only way forward if we don't want that bitter pill to consume our lives with pain and resentment. Over the years, we have trusted and helped so many people who have then repaid us by stealing, or betraying our trust in some way. (On one occasion, I did my nightly rounds to find the children had no blankets on their beds, only a top sheet. On investigation, a women who I had offered a job to because she was in desperate need, had stolen the lot!)

It isn't right, and we don't like it, but if we did not offer forgiveness to that person for the offence, we had better pack up and go home, as these people one day will have to be accountable to God for their actions of stealing from our children. This is God's mission, not an earthly mission, and as stewards, the onus of accountability falls squarely on our shoulders if we want to hear those treasured words "Well done, good and faithful servant" (Mathew 25:21).

If you can learn to forgive, your life will be deeply enriched.

CHAPTER TWENTY-FOUR
THE MOVE TO THE PLAINS

Our work was already becoming known, and young people were asking if they could volunteer with us. Accommodation to house them was limited, so we made a decision that we would rent some property on the plains and not located on the mountain. I named the five bed roomed detached house 'Pilgrim House.'

Staying with me in my room on the mountain was a little boy of four years of age who was HIV/AIDS positive, and the hospital had already informed me was terminally ill. He was visibly declining by the day. He still enjoyed sucking on a lollypop, and although he couldn't walk in his weakened state and had to be carried everywhere, he was still very much alert. I made the decision that I would take him to the airport with me to watch the airplane land and greet our two new arrivals. He would enjoy getting ready, putting new clothes on, and riding in a car. We met Jake and Daniel at the airport, and the journey to Pilgrim House only took a matter of minutes to reach our new accommodation. As the electricity had not yet been re-connected to the bungalow, we all sat and enjoyed a meal by candlelight.

During the night, the child began to cry, and I knew his time to leave us was not far off. As dawn broke, I wrapped the now unconscious child in a thick blanket and ventured out into the drizzling rain with an umbrella to wait for a dala dala to take me to the nearest hospital.

The child died in my arms en-route to the hospital.

For Jake and Daniel, the impact of this little boy's death, within hours of their arrival in Tanzania, left them with an emotional attachment to the needs of the poor and suffering. One of them, Jake, came to have a 'heart for Africa.' Daniel returned two years later and asked me if he could join a Maasai out-reach medical dispensary which was being held in a Maasai village, to which I agreed, and on his return, he had made the wonderful decision to become a doctor and this is now his chosen profession. Jake lives in USA / Uganda and has become a well-known photo-journalist. He works with 'big named' charities, who may require documentaries to be made or reporting on the African way of life.

Only God knows the unimaginable seeds that are planted through the lives of our precious children. So many of our volunteers profess to us that they now see things completely differently. They have a new understanding of the needs of a developing country. Their visit has been such 'a positive' experience for them, and they will never be the same again.

My perspective on the volunteers who join us on this mission is that I am 'sold out' on the youth of today. They make sacrifices to enable them to volunteer with us, perhaps not only studying at university during the day but also taking on two part-time jobs to pay for their flights. They have hearts of compassion and service to make a difference in the lives of our children and the community at large, and for that we bless them and salute them for their loving hearts.

After I had made all the arrangements for the funeral, I returned to the center to tell the staff of the demise of our little one. (We had no telephone, and the mobile network had not arrived as yet) When I walked through the gates of the home, and although I was greeted with children hanging on to my skirt and all clamoring to be picked up, I sensed in my spirit that something was missing. I could not feel the movement of the Holy Spirit in the center. I slowly spun around trying to pick some emotions up, but there was none.

The center was cold.

Within seven days, we had left the mountain and moved to the plains.

The property that we had occupied for over three years now lies derelict once again.

The children that came into care from this time on the mountain are now in their twenties. These are my first fruits. Our four eldest are now in colleges one to become a Teacher, another to become a Social Worker, one with such high grades in Biology and Physics can be a Doctor if he so chooses, and my oldest boy is at college to become a Business Administrator.

I look back and can see that this was the time that "God turned the heat up" in my life to allow me to be refined as silver (Psalm 66:10) in the fire, to enable all the 'gunk' in my life to float to the surface and be 'skimmed off', and for my faith to be increased in total dependence on His provision for all of our needs.

When I decided to offer this manuscript up for publication, I decided to do some 'information gathering' before I proceeded any further.

I was surprised to find that 800 published books come onto the market each day and the library shelf life of a book is just ten years. These facts set me thinking that the Holy Bible, which was written some two thousand years ago and is still a No. 1 best seller, has to have been "God breathed" for it to have lasted so long. It has stood the test of time.

The move from the mountain to the plains resulted in another rented accommodation which we named Malaika house (house of the angels). The property that we acquired had stood empty for over ten years, and it needed a full re-paint and some modernization before we could start to call it home.

We now had two homes, Pilgrim House and Malaika House. As the number of children increased, (one day we were asked by social welfare to receive 24 children in one day) we made the decision that Pilgrim House would be the boys' home and Malaika the home for the girls. For a couple of years we just 'growed and growed'.

We also opened a Saturday morning "Kid's Club" where we provided a good nourishing meal and seminars on hygiene and other relevant issues to the local children. We also would give away any clothes that we had spare as some of these children looked quite neglected, and we offered to pay school fee's where we found the parents to be too poor to even purchase a school uniform for their child. We were also able to monitor any child that we thought might be vulnerable and need to be brought into our full-time care from off the streets.

On this one occasion, our store manager, when she brought the cooked food to the club for distribution, burst into tears. I went over to see why she was crying. She told me that she had heard a rumor that there was a child locked in a hut and being left to die by his father, but she didn't know where it was. All that she knew was that it was in an isolated place, and she didn't know how to help the child. Comforting her, I said that I would call for our nurse to come to the club, then when we closed at 3:00 p.m., we would get into the car and go search for the hut.

I had been driving and searching in the vicinity where our manager thought the hut might be for well over an hour but still we found no clue as to the huts whereabouts, and everyone we asked 'knew nothing'. I turned the car off the main road and crossed a river bed which was dry, and as I 'geared up' to climb the bank on the other side, there was a herder standing over his dying cow which had insufficient strength to climb up the bank and had fallen over in its weakened state due to the existing drought. We travelled the mud road for a further fifteen minutes and saw nothing but burnt ochre fields, and then as I drove further on along a ridge top, we spotted a mud / stick hut stood by itself in the middle of a field. "There!" "Over their" the manager yelled, "that must be it!" I drove over the field to this isolated hut which was as big as a goat pen and the three of us got out of the car and walked over to the hut. We tried to look through the cow dung that filled the gaps but it was too dark to see, I pushed some dung into the hut with my finger to try to look inside, but it was still pitch black, just as we had decided that this couldn't be the place, we heard a small murmur coming from inside the hut. Our store manager, turned on her heels, and picked up a hand-sized rock went over to the padlock on the hut door and smashed the lock open with vengeance. She opened the door and stooped in with the nurse and I following her, our eyes having to adjust to the darkness we heard a little murmur again in the far corner of the hut, we were appalled to see the outline of a small boy laying on some dirty rags, laying in his body fluids, his legs had sores down both sides and were in a 'scissor' position, his head had an open wound where he had continually rubbed it against a piece of wood and he was terribly emaciated. Nurse moved forward and gathered the scrap of humanity into her arms and walked out of the hut into the bright sunlight. The child started to whimper because of the sunshine in his eyes, so our store manager removed her kanga (piece of material) that was wrapped around her waist, and covered the child with it, I returned to the car to fetch the First Aid Kit and my bottle of water which the nurse used to wet the lips of the child and to gently start to clean between his sore legs. I immediately rang our social worker and asked him to get in a taxi and get to us 'pronto,' and I handed the phone to our manager for her to try to describe where we actually where. Sam arrived, and we explained all that we knew. His long strides told us that he was feeling the emotional anguish that we all felt as he headed off towards where the 'ten-cell' leader lived for an explanation as to who and why had this disabled child been locked in a hut and left to die. He arrived back with a group of people, and as soon as he had gathered all the necessary information that he required for his report, we all got back into the car knowing full well that we would have to pay a visit to the police station to receive a recorded number before we could take the child to hospital.

On the return journey, the manager spotted a man walking along the road. "That's the father," she exclaimed, pointing her finger towards the man. 'I'm sure of it. Sam, who was now driving my vehicle stopped the car and jumped out, and approached the man. "Are you the father of this child?" he asked. "Yes," replied the man, and he took hold of the man and placed him in the back of the Serf. Sam drove straight to the police station without saying another word. He parked the car and got out and went straight inside the station. A few minutes later, he came outside with a police officer.

As I was sat next to the window nursing the child and knew the police officer, he smiled and waved to me as they both approached the car. Sam opened my side door, and I removed the kanga that was covering the child. I can still recall the shock – horror on the face of the police officer at seeing the child for the first time. The officer turned and asked the father if this child was his son, and he replied, "yes". The officer then grabbed his shirt at the shoulders and 'soldier like' quickly marched the father into the police station. I was anxious to get the child to the hospital, and it seemed ages before Sam re-appeared with the recorded number. He started the car engine, and we proceeded on the thirty minute journey to the hospital. "What was that noise we heard?" I asked. "Don't ask," he responded abruptly, and silently concentrated on his driving again.

After we had been underway for about fifteen minutes, Sam did reveal that the officer started to write out the father's charge sheet, and when he asked the father the name of the child, he said, "he couldn't remember." This brought an instant reaction from the officer that a father couldn't remember the name of his own child.

The father was released from custody after three days, and no charges were brought against him.

I named the boy Abraham, and he has lived within our care for the last nine years. Abraham has cerebral palsy and is what we call 'high maintenance' as our carers have to see to all of his needs, but he can laugh and smile, and he knows my voice when I enter our 'special needs' facility. When I'm enjoying time out in my potting shed, I will place Abraham in a special reclining wheelchair that we have and take him into the outdoor shed with me where we listen to music and I 'chat' to him as I re-pot or take cuttings. The credit is mostly due to our staff, who when he was released after two months in hospital, cared for him and made the child thrive so well.

CHAPTER TWENTY-FIVE
A PRISON VISIT

ince my six month stay in Portugal in 1999 where I was really 'set on fire' by the Holy Spirit, I had brought that gift with me to Africa where I was often able to see pictures in my 'mind's eye' and intrinsically know that the picture in some way was to either encourage someone or for me to act upon it.

One morning in prayer, I received a 'mind's eye' picture of a group of women seated upon the ground, and they were all wearing orange overalls. At the side of the women were officers wearing khaki uniforms and holding a baton underneath their arms. The picture moved on to the second stage and I saw myself bending down and offering to these ladies a small tub of margarine. The tubs were so small that they were just made for poor people who had too little money to purchase the larger containers that we purchased to spread on the children's bread. The picture then disappeared. "I wondered what that means" I thought, as I wrote it down in my journal. It must have something to do with a prison as I have seen prisoners wearing the regulatory orange uniforms when they pass by in a prison vehicle.

Six weeks later, I am handed a plastic bag full of small tubs of margarine which has been donated by a shopkeeper. "So, Lord, if I understand this message correctly, you want me to go to a women's prison and give the women who were sat on the ground a small tub of margarine, and then what? You do know that when I tell the staff

A LIGHT IN AFRICA

where I'm intending on going there is going to be ructions." "This should really be interesting," I thought as I already knew the response that I would get from the staff at any mention of a prison, let alone to actually visit one. I considered that I would have to play my cards close to my chest and only inform the staff on a "need to know basis" where we were actually going. I researched where the nearest ladies prison was and called for the vehicle to come and pick-me up. I invited a staff member and our nurse to accompany me in the vehicle without actually explaining to them where we were going. Whilst living in the UK, I had heard that prisons were like 'holiday camps,' but in Tanzania it was a very much a fear-based institution.

We all trundled into the 'ladybird' which was a second-hand pick-up truck that we had painted red to hide all the rust marks, and the children thought that it was quite 'neat' to have a name for a vehicle.

Four Maasai warriors, who were used as security, jumped over the tailboard in to the back of the pick-up thinking we were going out on a jolly, and we moved off down the road. Then the dreaded question was asked, "Where did you say we were going?" I explained the best that I could about the picture and the tubs of margarine. "Surely mama, you must have it all wrong. God would never ask you to go inside a prison, for they're dangerous places full of diseases." I noticed the car started to slow down as the brake was applied for some reason. And then another question: "But mama, you don't mean to say we are going right this minute, do you?" "Well I think it's a good a time as any to try to un-ravel what plans God has for these women, 'don't you?" Silence was the loud response as the vehicle came to a halt along the road. A Maasai head came through the side window enquiring why had we stopped and where were we going. "Gereza," (prison) came back the reply. The question was asked again, and the same answer given: "Gereza." With that, the four Maasai jumped off the back of the truck one-by-one and were seen running down the road.

The silence that enveloped the cab was as if all the air had been sucked out and we were now sitting in a vacuum as each of us wondered what was going to happen.

152

We arrived at the prison gates, and the guard came over to ask the purpose of our business. I leant forward and said I was looking to meet with the Prison Commander. The gates were opened, and we were waved in. I knew the two staff members were feeling pretty fearful about this, and I started to have a guilty conscience that they were both unwilling victims to a situation that they couldn't comprehend, and by the end of the day, they could well be "guilty by association with mama Lynn."

I made a comment on how lovely the fields looked with all the vegetables the prisoners were growing. No response. The car pulled up in front of a wall, and the handbrake was applied. As the two sat mutely beside me, I made the suggestion that I think we should pray and offer the following couple of hours into the hands of God. After I prayed, I indicated that I would now like to leave the vehicle please. The nurse opened the door, got out to allow me to exit, and then promptly got back in to the car and closed the door.

I walked over to the information desk, and I asked an officer if it would be possible for me to meet with the Prison Commander. He pointed to a bench for me to sit upon, and I went to the door and waved for my two reluctant colleagues to get out of the car and follow me.

Twenty minutes passed before the officer returned and beckoned us to follow him. We halted at a door, and I was intrigued to see how the officer knocked. Europeans tend to knock on a door with their hand straight in front of them. Tanzanians knock with their palms upwards. The officer listened closely to the door for the response to the knock. He opened the door and stood aside to allow the three of us entry into the room.

My first impression was one of surprise. The room was very long, and it had the largest full length polished table that I had ever seen. A further table ran horizontally to it and sitting in a very large chair was a very impressive looking man in uniform. Praying a quick 'arrow prayer', I walked over to the man. Smiling I held out my hand and said, "Good morning, Sir. My name is mama Lynn of Light in Africa's Children's Homes." "Yes, I know you," he said smiling and shook my hand. "You do, sir?" I said somewhat taken aback. "Yes," we have met on a previous occasion." "We have?" I meekly responded, trying to desperately remember where I had met this officer before. Seeing my confusion, he replied, "The last time we met, I asked you what you were doing with all those children." Clarity came in a rush as I remembered. "You were sat at a table drinking a soda, when I arrived with about twenty children on a social outing, and you asked me 'where had all these children come from?' Yes, now I remember, and as we chatted, I asked you what you did for a living and you told me you were an askari (soldier). You didn't tell me you where the Commander of the Prison Service!" He sat back in his huge chair and laughed as he motioned for us to sit down. As I sat and surveyed my surroundings, I just gave God the glory. "God You are utterly amazing. You have already opened the door for me. All You wanted me to do was to have the faith to walk through it."

"How can I help you, mama Lynn? Have you come to visit a prisoner?" he asked. "No, not exactly. I have come to ask permission to see many female prisoners. It is a little complicated, but if you will allow me to explain the picture that I have received in my 'mind's eye' and that I felt that God was leading me to this prison for a particular reason. But what that reason is, I have to be honest, I really do not know. Is it possible for me to give your female prisoners a small tub of margarine?" "No, not really," came back the reply because we usually don't give our prisoners bread you see" he responded. In an act of divine inspiration, I responded, "Oh the margarine is not for the bread. The margarine is for mixing with the porridge in the morning." He hesitated and thought through the implications of my request. "Well, that's fine then, when did you want to visit? "How many females are we looking at to receive this gift?" I asked. He consulted with the officer who had been standing to attention throughout this dialogue with his Commander, and a number was given. "Can we come in the morning around 10:00 a.m.? That should give us sufficient time to purchase some more of the small tubs of margarine." We shook hands and left the room. During the whole of the ten minute interview, the limited amount of conversation by my two accompanying colleagues had been clearly noticed by me! They walked quickly to the truck, got in, and started the vehicle, thankful that they were on their way home to see their families and their worst nightmare was over.

The following day after visiting many local small village one room shops, we eventually was satisfied that we had enough of the tubs to give to the prisoners, and we made our way back to gereza.

We were escorted to where the women were housed, and we were meticulously searched and our bags were emptied and checked. Even some random packs of margarine tubs had the foil removed to ensure nothing had been hidden inside, and our impression was of a very well-run prison service. A female officer showed us to a small door which had a high step, and we had to duck down low to enter through it. When I straightened up, I stood and stared, at the scene before my eyes, for there was the exact picture that I had seen in my 'mind's eye' picture some weeks previous. The women were sitting on the grass in there orange overalls and female officers in there khaki uniforms were at the side of them with their batons under their arms. The only piece of the picture that was missing was me giving out the tubs of margarine. I was shown over to a podium, and I stood there looking at this amazing scene, and thought, "How does all this work? How can I see something and then it to actually happen so clearly weeks later?"

"Good morning, ladies," I began, "I want to tell you something very important. You need to know that I have seen you before any of you have seen me here today. I saw you all sitting on the grass exactly how you are today, and that was about six weeks ago. I have been very kindly allowed by your Commanding Officer to fulfill God's mission today by coming to visit with you." (I still at this point had no idea as to why I was there, but all that I knew was that I had to give each one of these ladies a tub of margarine) "You need to know," I continued, that I am not a preacher women or an evangelist. I am just a simple women who loves the Lord, and was asked by God to come here to Tanzania and help the children who were dying of the HIV/AIDS virus, especially in this area. Light in Africa has many children in its care who are being well taken care of and provided for by the benevolence of God Himself. I would like today to bring you a word from the Holy Scriptures. (Mathew 25:36)

"I was hungry and you gave me some food

I was thirsty and you game me a drink,

I was a stranger and you took me in.

Naked and you clothed me,

In prison and you visited with me."

"Ladies, Jesus, is visiting with you here today in this prison."

(This brought much noise and clapping.)

I left the podium and collected the first bag of margarine and began to distribute it first to the officers standing around the prisoners – today in God's presence everyone was loved and a child of God, and it was important to me to show them the respect that they deserved - and then to the ladies sitting down along the first row. Each time I passed a tub over I would say, "Mungu Akurbiriki (God Bless You). It was only when I had reached the middle of the row about eight rows deep, that I sensed the reason as to why I was there. I stopped, and circled slowly around, then around again. Silence fell as everyone watched and wondered what I was doing. "There is someone around me here for who, like in Revelations Chapter 3:20, Jesus is standing at the door of her heart and knocking to gain entry, but she is resisting the offer of His love. I urge you dear lady to accept Salvation. My Jesus is a gentleman, and He will not come into your heart unless you personally invite Him in. That is why He has sent me here today. You wanted proof, here I am on His behalf." At this comment, there was much excitement and finger pointing to a lady sitting close by my feet. The prison officers took a step closer to the ladies, and I moved on and completed my assignment of distributing the tubs. I then went back to the podium, when a mature prisoner asked for permission to stand up and speak from a prison officer. This was granted, and she began. "Mama, on behalf of the ladies in this prison today, we want to thank you for being a faithful servant of God. What you have said is all very true and a great encouragement to us in our faith. Thank you for taking care of our children. Now I would like to bring you a word from the bible, and that is Philippians 4:13: "It is God who strengthens you.""

I thanked them all, giving words of encouragement to stay strong in the faith, and we left the courtyard.

The whole process had taken less than 50 minutes, but God only knows what seeds was planted during that day.

CHAPTER TWENTY-SIX
A MIRACLE RESCUE

(Please do not read this story if you are of a sensitive nature.)

I awoke to the many sounds of the children preparing to get ready for breakfast. Squeals came from the shower room as the cold shower water hit them, intermingled with snatches of praise songs, and arguments about who had taken whose dress and was wearing it, on this one particular Sunday morning.

I dressed and entered the main lounge of Malaika House and was shocked to see a room full of police officers at 7am in the morning. As I closed the door behind me, emotional panic flooded my nervous system as I thought the police were here once again responding to a closure order issued by 'the thorn in my side.' I put on a smile and greeted the officers warmly with a "good morning officers," and both male and female officers in uniform responded their greeting in unison. "Shikamoo mama," they said. "Marahaba," I replied. One female officer got up out of the chair that she had been sitting in and walked towards me holding something in her hand. She was obviously offering me something, and I held out my hands to receive a piece of material, but when I had it in my hands, the material was wet and warm. As I held the bundle, the officer started to peel the material away to reveal a naked baby. First impression told me, when my eyes saw the state that this baby was in, was she had little to no chance of survival. The eye lids were swollen and closed. The umbilical cord had feces around it, and I immediately thought of Tetanus / Lockjaw as a condition the baby might succumb to, and from the waist down the skin was red. I looked up at the officer for an explanation. This is the story of how this naked baby came into the care of Light in Africa.

A mother on Mount Kilimanjaro gave birth to a baby, and for whatever reason we shall never know, decided to dispose of the child. She placed the placenta into a plastic bag, and holding the baby, she found a pit latrine (6' drop toilet) and dropped both the baby and the placenta into the pit latrine. The first that happened was that the pit was full of sewerage and was due to be emptied the following week. If it had already been emptied, the baby girl would have dropped straight to the bottom and no-one would have known that she was there. The second miracle was that the home that the mother had chosen to use for the disposal of her baby belonged to an elderly couple who had their grand-daughter staying with them for the weekend. In the middle of the night, the teenager decided she needed to go down the path to use the outside toilet. Whilst there, she heard a noise coming from the pit and rushed back into her grandparents home and woke them up to say, "There's a baby in the toilet." Not dismissing their grandchild that she must have been dreaming and to go back to bed, the grandparents got out of bed, took a torch and walked down the path to the toilet. The grandfather removed the two planks of wood that they stood on to defecate and shone the torch onto the face of the baby. The grandfather went off to fetch a rato (a three pronged gardening tool), and rolling up, his sleeves he placed the rato through the handles of the plastic bag and grabbing hold of the baby's arm, he pulled the two separate parts up together from out of the sewage. When the baby was laid on terra firma, the grandmother dashed off to find some camba (string) to tie the umbilical cord with and cut the baby free of the placenta. As soon as that was done she wrapped the baby in a kanga, and they walked down the mountain in the dark to the police stand.

All thirteen police officers who were on-duty wanted to be part of bringing the baby to LIA. The lady officer had one request of me before they departed: Would I please baptize the baby as they knew the likely hood was that the baby would not survive? I agreed and went into the kitchen to ask the staff to make tea and sandwiches for the officers and to give me two candles and a bowl. As I held the baby in my arms to take her to the table which had become a make-shift alter, I prayed that she would survive and become a testament of God's good grace, and I sensed that one day she would become the 'hope' of Africa. After the ceremony, I handed the baby over to our LIA doctor and nurse who had been called earlier to come and attend to the child, not knowing if I would see the child alive again.

Eight months later, the child had become a beautiful little girl as she sat amongst her peer group playing with her toys in our nursery dressed in a white satin dress and hat. Her future adoptive mother visited us that one particular day and fell in love with her.

This 'miracle' child who beat all the odds of survival, was later adopted and now lives 'happily' in Tanzania with her parents.

CHAPTER TWENTY-SEVEN
ALLERGIC REACTION

After living on the foothills of Mount Kilimanjaro for three years with the Chagga tribe and our subsequent move to the plains to a place called Bomang'ombe which in Kiswahili means the 'house of the cows' which is situated just twenty minutes from the main Kilimanjaro International Airport and after the move to flat ground, I found that my health began to deteriorate, which up to that time, had remained quite good except for one bad bout of malaria. The symptoms started with just a cough, which became very persistent, and progressed to an unshakable heavy chest cold. A visit for a check-up at a hospital to rule out all of the nasties left me with bags of antibiotics but no firm diagnoses or conclusion as to the problem.

I then experienced breathing difficulties and visited different specialists including one to test if I was allergic to something, - perhaps children - but all to no avail, my condition deteriorated further and became life threatening. On one occasion, I was being taken to the airport dispensary gasping for breath when our nurse had to stop the car, rush into a pharmacy, purchase a syringe and adrenalin shot to keep me going until I arrived at the facility where I was dragged up to the first floor stairs to a hospital bed where the airport doctor managed to slowly give me an injection and brought me around.

An English couple, who had lived in Tanzania for forty odd years working in the hospitality environment, suggested I travelled to Arusha to meet with the doctor of whom they had known for many years. Once again, tests where completed, and the doctor had some sobering news for me. I had asthma and for my survival I should leave the area where I was living. I protested that I had never suffered with asthma the whole of my life, so why now? A question of course the doctor could not answer. I left his surgery with a heavy heart. Was God asking me to leave the children and either go back to the UK or to another country? The amount of time that I was now spending in bed allowed me plenty of prayer time to try to find out.

Two days after the doctor's visit, I had another bad asthma attack and found great difficulty in breathing. LIA's doctor placed an IV in my arm, and as I watched the flow of the drip into my arm, I wondered what was happening to me. Was this a 'spiritual attack' I was experiencing? Mama Coupa came into the room and asked if I would like a cup of tea, and said there was a Pastor from the UK in the lounge asking if he could see me before he left for the airport to take a flight back to the UK. The bottle had around a quarter of the contents left and I asked her to make him a cup of tea and as soon as it was completed, I would get dressed and meet with him.

The Pastor had heard about the work of LIA, and as he had some time to spare before his flight departed, he thought he would just ' pop-in' to hear more of what the Lord was doing in Tanzania. I explained the best I could in between gasps for breath, and he made a remark that perhaps my time here was now completed and God needed me to leave to go somewhere else. The Pastor left, and I returned to my bed. I now had a confirmation of what the doctor had said to me earlier, and I dozed off to sleep from sheer exhaustion.

In my half-awake sleep state, I could see a large derelict building which was the one my eyes were always drawn to when I travelled to Moshi on the dala dala. I always looked to see if there were any people moving about inside of it, but never actually saw anyone. The picture then moved to an empty cement swimming pool, and down the pool were some cracks from top-to-bottom. I could see it very clearly, then I awoke. I lay in bed wondering what all of this meant. Coupa came in and wanted to know what I would like to have for lunch. I asked her if she knew who that big house near Moshi belonged to which had stood empty for many years, and she said she didn't know. "Would you try to find out?" I asked. "I'm going to Moshi tomorrow. I will see what I can find out for you," she said.

After a week of investigation, she had found the names of the trustees of the building and an interview was arranged. After that, a contract was drawn up by our lawyer, and I asked him to make it 'sound' for the five year period with all the 'I's dotted and the 'T's crossed that when we started to spend money on renovation work and improve the property, the Trustees would not come along and want an increase in rent that had happened to us on a previous occasion with another landlord.

The contract was signed by the Executive Committee, and the keys were handed over to mama Coupa. Feeling a little better, and having not driven the car for some time, I put two five year olds into the car, and with Coupa and the keys, we decided to go and have a look around our third property, and make notes of what refurbishments were required after the building had stood empty for over twenty years.

Coupa went upstairs to look into the many bedrooms, and I and the two children decided we would take a look downstairs. I opened a door and found the room quite dark so I went over to a window that had been secured with a piece of hardboard. I took hold of it with both hands and pulled as hard as I could. The next moment, I found myself flying through the air, somersaulting and falling down hard on to a corner of a cement block. Dazed, all I could hear were these two little voices saying to me 'pole sana mama' 'pole sana'. (sorry mama, sorry). As the pain hit my hip, I asked the children to go find mama Coupa and bring her to me. She came in at a run, and she saw me lying splayed on my back. "Mama, mama" she cried, "What can I do." "Call for someone to come and collect the car. I won't be able to drive. I could have broken my hip." The pain was excruciating as I was gently pulled to my feet, and with support, I hobbled to the car. An X-ray was taken, and I had not broken my hip. When our nurse looked at the X-ray, she could not believe how everything was 'mushed up' inside but on the outside there was not one bruise. This 'accident,' which our superstitious staff was convinced was either satanic or witchdoctor induced, kept me in bed for a further month before I left to live in this very large property. As I walked around another property attached to the land, I saw the swimming pool with the cracks going down it, so I knew I was in the right place where God wanted me to be, and quite unbelievably, I have never had another asthma attack since.

CHAPTER TWENTY-EIGHT
LIVING AT THE WHITE HOUSE

Throughout the years, we have hosted a great many overseas volunteers. From large private school groups, students from universities, social welfare and medical student's working on their electives, gap year students, small groups, couples who may have decided to 'do something' different by giving back a little, to retirees who have a vast wealth of experience to offer to our mission. They all come with a willingness to make a difference in our children's lives and that of the tribes where we live.

Many returning volunteers cannot believe the great strides that we have made over the years that they have been away, but I tell them, "God is always on the move. Like the seasons, nothing stays the same with Him, and sometimes I have such a job just to keep up with the ideas He plants in my mind. A few years ago, a small church group from America came to volunteer with LIA and asked if they could work on a small construction job. I asked the five men if they would like to build a 'Jungle Gym' for our children, to which they readily agreed.

On Monday morning, construction plans were made, and the men went off to Moshi to purchase the wood and materials that they would need to build the piece of strong equipment. The following day, as the men were busily working, hammering and sawing the wood, I decided to take them out a tray of tea and biscuits (Always the English women). As I approached the area, I noticed that one young man had a black sling supporting his arm, and he was having great difficulty hammering a nail into a piece of wood with the other hand. "What have you done to your arm?" I asked him as I placed the tray down on a piece of wood. "I fell and injured it, but in two month's time I am having a fusion operation on my wrist. All my bones in my fingers in this hand are dead after the accident, and the surgeon is going to operate on my wrist to fuse the nerves together. If this operation fails, it doesn't bear thinking about what the next stage will be." I chatted a little more with the men who had stopped work to drink the tea, and returned with the tray to the kitchen.

The following day, as I walked down a side path, I noticed one of our six year old boys hitting a little girl. I went over to the crying girl and asked the boy to apologize and for the little girl to forgive him his meanness and asked him not to continue with this unkind behavior. Thinking no more about the incident, I carried on with my daily chores. The following day, I came down the staircase to see the same little boy this time beating a dog with a stick! This behavior was now too much, and I had to take action. Taking the stick out of his hand and breaking it over my knee, without a word to him I waltzed him in to the store room in the kitchen. "OK, on your knees. Let us pray about this bad behavior. I knelt down beside the boy and started to pray about his behavior. As I was in 'mid-flow,' I saw in my 'mind's eye' the young man with the sling on his arm, and I had a sense that God was going to heal his hand. I didn't know how, but just a sense the hand was going to be healed. I finished the prayer and asked the child to go and play and be a kinder boy or no-one would want to play with him, and he skipped off. I went over to talk to the young man. "Will you do something for me please?" I asked. "I will if I can," the young man replied. "I want you to each day, right up to when you go into hospital for the operation, to lift up your bad hand with your good hand, and bless someone with your bad hand." "Can you repeat that to me again," the young man said, looking quizzical. "Yes. Every day, with your good hand, I want you to lift up your bad hand and give a blessing to someone." He performed a demonstration of lifting his hand up to bless somebody. "Do you think you can do that for me?" I asked. "Yes. I can do that. Every day until I go in to hospital?" "Yes. Good," I said, leaving without giving the young man any inclination as to why I had asked him to perform this daily task.

Two months later, I journeyed to Moshi to do some internet work at Dot Café where I had been friends with Deshant, his brother Nictesh, their mum, and their families since I arrived in Tanzania, and when I opened up the internet site, I was surprised to see an email from this young man. It read something like this... "Mama Lynn, I can hardly write this email to you for the tears that are flooding down my cheeks. I was admitted into the hospital for the 'fusion' operation and was asked to have tests done before tomorrow's operation. Yesterday, I had X-rays, and today the surgeon asked me to have an ultra-sound to enable him to get a good picture of my wrist during the operation. The surgeon has just stood in front of me, with hands shaking, holding the scan and said he doesn't know what has happened. My hand is totally healed and my fingers are alive and not dead, and tomorrow all he will be doing is taking out the pins, and not performing the 'fusion' operation. Glory to God."

Three months later, I visited the young man in America, and shook his once injured hand. He had now gone back to work and everything was as it should be. "Keep giving God the Glory and blessing people," I said as he left to go to work. I really believe, when he is a somewhat more mature Christian, this young man's hand is going to be a powerful instrument for God's work.

CHAPTER TWENTY-NINE
LOCKED IN STIGMATISATION

Over the years, with overseas donor countries placing large amounts of funding and emphasis on education regarding the HIV/AIDS virus, the situation that I see from a 'grass root' perspective is that ideas that people once had about the virus are now slowly starting to change. There are still 'pockets' of resistance and, adults and children still have to accept 'name calling' which can and does cause our staff problems with our fifty three children in care who are carrying the virus when either they refuse to take their prescribed medication (because nobody else has to take it, why should I?) resulting in hospital admission, or they return home crying because a child has called them a 'bad' name.

Stigmatization is a painful thing to bear, and it is sometimes hard to understand the mindset of people who resort to it.

My oldest granddaughter and I were shopping in a supermarket one day, and I was at one end of the store with my hand in a freezer purchasing some frozen fish and Grace was standing near the counter. Now as Grace had lived in Tanzania for five years and spoke fluent Kiswahili, she was 'privy' to a conversation between two teenage girls. Grace shouts to me, "Nana, is it OK if I get a dollar voucher for my mobile?" "Yes. Of course it is," I responded. "Ask check-out to put it on my account." The two young girls waiting in the queue next to Grace whispered to each other in Kiswahili. "Don't stand near that mzungu (European). She can only afford a one dollar voucher on her mobile, and if we touch her we will contract her poverty." And that is one of the problems of why we only receive a small amount of Tanzanians who actually want to volunteer with us. They are afraid that if they come into close contact with our children who have the virus or a disability or work with the poor on our medical out-reach programs that they are going to be like some of these people we serve, or that in the future they may have a disabled child or that they too will one day be poor. Again, I believe it is only time and education that is going to change these out-dated ideas. Here are three stories which highlight the effects of stigmatization.

I was called to meet a hospital social worker who was waiting for me in our lounge area, and another lady and a boy of around six years of age was also with her. After the usual salutation, we walked over to a distant table to talk. The aunt was sitting at the other table with the child. She had inherited the boy after his parents had both died of AIDS. She took him home with her after the funeral but refused to have the child living in the same house as her, so she placed him outside in a chicken coup to live with the chickens. As the child became terminally ill, the aunt decided to take him to the local hospital, and when the child was being examined, he told the doctor that he refused to go back home with the aunt because she gave him no food and beat him, and he was living with the chickens. At this accusation, the doctor brought in the hospital social worker who had brought him to LIA to see if we would care for the child, which we readily agreed to. For four days, the little boy was shown lots of loving kindness, and I know of one particular volunteer from Iowa who would sneak into his bedroom and treat him to a supply of chocolates, something that he had never enjoyed before, but then his condition became serious and he was taken into hospital for treatment. An LIA carer stayed with him in the hospital, and when his uncle went to visit him, he refused to see or speak to him. What strong conviction the little boy had to have to be able to say no. He died three days later.

The Manager of a children's home about fifteen miles from where we lived came to visit with me and to ask for help with a problem that he had and this is his story: He had been asked by another children's home to take in a girl of about seven /eight years of age, but when the trustees of the home where he was a manager found out the child was HIV/AIDS positive, they told the manager that they could not keep the child in the center and he would have to find another place for the child to live. Three homes had now refused to keep the child, we welcomed her with open arms as we feel it is our honor and duty to help God's suffering children. After all, that is what I was brought from the UK to Africa to do.

After a couple of months of Rosalind staying with us, a woman arrived with a small boy saying that she was the mother of the child. Our Social worker was interested to know "why the mother wasn't caring for the child herself." "Because she's infected," said the mother. "Have you and the child been tested?" the social worker asked the mother. "No, we don't have it, only her," said the mother. Feeling pressured, the mother got up and left. Our social worker, along with the manager from the other children's home, and myself decided we would go and see the mother in her own home, and try to counsel her as to the need for her and the boy to get tested, and if necessary, receive treatment, especially for the young boy. First, we visited the home of a Pastor and his wife who told us that they had allowed the women and boy to live in a wooden lean-to because the woman had no-where else to live. The Pastor then showed us around the back of their house to where the mother and boy were living. Again, the woman was urged to seek medical treatment for her and the boy. She continued to refuse. Here was a mother in total denial that she had the HIV/AIDS virus or that she had given it to her oldest child.

Another two months later, and the mother arrived again at the home. We served the mother and the boy lunch, and asked if she had decided to be tested. She again repeated that she wasn't positive because she was feeling so well, so why should she undergo such degradation of a blood test. I was playing with the children on the swings when I saw Rosalind run into the bedrooms with a huge smile spread over her face, and as she disappeared, the mother and boy left through our security gate. I went into Rosalind's bedroom to find her trying to hurriedly fasten the back of her best white lacy dress while at the same time place her foot in a shoe. "Darling," I said, "your mama has already gone." The change on that poor child's face from sheer joy and excitement because her mother had said that she was going to take her home with her, to horror at the painful truth that she had just said that and didn't want her to go home with her is a picture that I will never forget. She burst into uncontrollable sobs of anguish which went on and on until she was totally spent, and I wrapped her in a blanket and laid with her until she fell asleep exhausted. We had many medical volunteers staying with us from the UK universities at that time, and they did their very best to ensure Rosalind knew she was loved and cared for. They were there to hold her hand when a drip was running and to make her smile and laugh, and hand her different colors as she crayoned in a book knowing that her body was deteriorating fast in its weakened state. We called her mother to come in the last two days of her life, just to be with her and try to give the child some comfort, and Rosalind was yet another child that died in my arms.

The mother and the young boy later tested positive, and we offered the mother a job and a place to live with her child. She returned the favor by appropriating funds that didn't belong to her and was later dismissed.

CHAPTER THIRTY
WHY WASTE FOOD?

I have a big problem with Christmas Eve. It's one of the busiest days in Light in Africa's yearly calendar as we prepare to ensure all the children in our care receive a present and a good Christmas lunch. Also the children that we feed at the daily Food Kitchen have their special party on Boxing Day with a gift of school supplies to allow them to start school all prepared with exercise books, pens, and pencils. This all takes quite a bit of organizing to purchase all the stores for the Xmas period, so it becomes a bit of a problem for me when my time is taken up with 'issues'. For example, one Christmas Eve, I received a notice that there was a package to be collected at our local post office where a kind soul from the USA had posted a parcel of twenty one back packs to enable our older children to take with them to boarding school. On arrival at the counter, I am asked by an official to pay $600.00 dollar duty or else he will sell the backpacks. There is no-way that I can pay this outrageous demand, so by the time I have visited his supervisor twice (because the first time he still refused to follow her instructions), I have lost five hours of my 'purchasing and wrapping time' and my son and daughter-in-law were called into 'save the day,' and we completed everything at 3 a.m. on Christmas day.

My third story of stigmatization happened one Christmas Eve at the White House. With our two other children's homes twenty five kilometers away, we had to make plans and preparations to ensure that the distribution of the presents ran like clockwork. My daughter arrived from giving some presents to some disabled children who were living at home on the mountain and brought back with her a young man of sixteen years of age who was painfully thin and very sick.

The story was that David's mother and father had already died of the virus and the child went to live on the mountain with his grandparents. The grandparents were poor peasants and in their minds it was a waste of food to feed the child as he was going to die anyway! David was helped into the car as we set off for the six kilometer drive to our local training hospital. I knew beyond a shadow of doubt that it was going to be a long night. After the initial blood tests, David's CD4 count registered 0.6, the lowest the doctor had ever registered (CD4 count allows the doctor to see the state of the immune system from a blood slide). A file was prepared, and we were taken up to the ward. The only problem was that all the beds were full, and so a stretcher was pulled out and placed in the corridor, next to all the other patients lying along the wall. A blanket was brought, and David settled down to sleep whilst I sat upright at the end of his stretcher/make-shift bed.

The wind was howling along the corridor as I looked at my watch. "It's now official," I thought. "It's Christmas Day! One minute past twelve o'clock." I then heard the click click of shoes walking quickly down the corridor, and a voice shouting "Mama Lynn! Mama Lynn!" I have been looking all over the hospital for you! I thought you would be on the children's ward," this white coated lady said as she stopped alongside the stretcher in front of me. "I'm on men's medical because the boy is sixteen years of age and not allowed on the children's ward," I said trying to recall who the women was since she obviously knew me. "I really need you to do something for me," she said. "What's that?" I replied somewhat suspiciously. "Three months ago, a women gave birth just outside of our hospital gates and died, and we have had her baby boy in the nursery ever since. The nurses have really grown attached to the child, but we have to place him in a home. Will you take him with you tomorrow? I thought quickly, and said, "I will do a trade with you." "What do you mean by a trade?" she replied. It is now officially Christmas Day which is a really a big, hard working day for me and the staff at Light in Africa, and I haven't had a wink of sleep. I will take your baby with me tomorrow morning if your social worker has signed all the necessary paperwork, on the condition you will give me another stretcher and a blanket so I can at least gain a few hours sleep." "It's a deal," and with that she turned on her heels and hurried away the way she came, later bringing me the 'goods.' Our male carer arrived at 7:30 a.m. to relieve me and to stay with the boy and arrange breakfast for him whilst I went down to the nursery to collect the baby boy.

The baby boy is now a happy seven year old and the young man was placed on the anti-retro drugs and now is a self-employed brick maker.

CHAPTER THIRTY-ONE
AN UNFAITHFUL
AND FEARFUL HEART

I watched as dawn broke, and the emerging view of the 'snow-capped' Mount Kilimanjaro from our balcony was spectacular as I walked away to start my 'prayer time'. I knelt down to pray, and I had nearly completed my supplications and prayers when I had a sense that God was asking me to go to a mining area and open a children's home close to where the mining community lived. Shocked at this sense and the implications of it, I immediately dismissed it with the thought, "God would never want me to go and live in such a notoriously dangerous place.'

Ten days later, my daughter returned from an educational trip to South Africa and walked into my bedroom. She greeted me with a 'hi' and then astounded me with a question: "Mum is God sending you to work at the mining area?" "What! Who told you that? I haven't said anything to anyone about that. How did you know?" Seeing my utter confusion and bewilderment, she continued. "Teachers and students were all gathered at this ACE (Accelerated Christian Education) conference center when we started to pray, and I just sensed that God was going to send you to the mines to do His work for Him there." "Oh dear God! Please, no! I wouldn't last a week there. Everybody knows what a bad place it is with the witchdoctors and criminals living there, and my skin is white. Please! Anything else, God! Send me to China, send me to India or Somalia, but please don't send me to the mines."

After a week of praying and pleading with God, I relented and did what I always do if I need to know for sure God's plans for me or for Light in Africa: I lay down a fleece, just like Gideon did in Judges 6:36-40 (36) Gideon said to God, If you will save Israel by my hand as you have promised(37) look, I will place a wool fleece on the threshing floor, if there is dew only on the fleece and all the ground is dry, then I will know that you will save Israel by my hand, as you said." (38) And that is what happened. Gideon rose early the next day; he squeezed the fleece and wrung out the dew – a bowlful of water. (39) Then Gideon said to God, "Do not be angry with me. Let me make just one more request. Allow me one more test with the fleece. This time make the fleece dry and the ground covered with dew" That night God did so only the fleece was dry; all the ground was covered with dew. (The NIV Study Bible)

"God if you really want me to go to the mines, then my fleece is this: "As You know, we do not have any vehicles. If you really need me to go to the mines, I will need a good, very strong vehicle, either for an 'emergency get-away' or to take a sick child to hospital. I leave this fleece in the throne room of heaven this August morning."

Two weeks prior to Christmas, I welcomed two visitors from America whom I had not met before. Over coffee, this mature couple told me that they had just sold their businesses and retired, and coming over to Africa was an answered wish that they had wanted to experience. During the conversation, the gentlemen just happened to say, "Mama Lynn, I don't see any vehicles here?" "Well," I replied, "that's because we don't have any!" "How do you do your work with no vehicles?" he asked. "Either we walk or we use the local dala dala transport," I replied. "The man looked at his wife and said, "Well, I think we and our church back home could possibly purchase you a vehicle. What would you like?" I thought I was going to have to pick myself up off the floor at this suggestion, but I responded with, "a double cab pick-up truck would be good. We could carry our children and our Monday morning stores in the back of the truck. Thank you." This kind couple actually purchased me a very strong 4x4 Toyota Surf which I knew was for me to go to the mines with. Behind the wheel, I did a few laps with all of the staff and family clapping. God had now answered my fleece with a good strong vehicle. But I was an unfaithful servant and made no effort to fulfill what God wanted of me. It was now April of the following year, eight months from when I received God's first request to go to help the children in the mining community. I was on tour in America, and I was staying at this lovely home of some friends, when I decided to take a shower and prepare what I was going to speak about at the meeting that I was invited to attend that evening. I dabbed on perfume from out of a bottle that had been provided for me, but as I didn't have any sense of smell, I think perhaps I could have gone a little 'overboard' with it, but I was relishing and enjoying the change of lifestyle from the austere life that I lived in Africa. Then from out of nowhere I was literally hit by the "Holy Spirit" and fell to the floor. As I laid there, I heard God's voice say, "While you are here enjoying yourself, I have children dying un-necessarily at the mining community."

I was in emotional turmoil and overpowered with remorse at my actions and unfaithfulness and burst into uncontrollable sobs. I cried and cried asking God to forgive me because He had been so faithful in my fleece by providing a car for me but I had totally disregarded His request because I had allowed fear to hold me in its clutches instead of leaning and believing in faith. I don't know how long I laid on the floor, but then I heard a knock on the door, and the lady of the house said, "Mama Lynn, it is time to go." "Yes" Lord, I promise you I will now do what has been asked of me." I slowly got-up from the floor and looked into the mirror. Red eyes stared back at me as I tried to gain some composure, how on earth could I possibly speak to people tonight about the work of Light in Africa? I would have to consider cancelling it. But I serve a faithful and forgiving God, and He had humbled me to my core. Therefore, I was able to stand and speak about this Amazing God that I now so humbly serve, and I learnt a valuable lesson.

On my return to Tanzania, my first job was to try to find out all the information that I would require to operate another children's home in a different region of Tanzania.

CHAPTER THIRTY-TWO
PILOT SCHEME

We now had all the necessary permission to work in a different area of Tanzania, and we were very impressed with the welcome that we had received from the local government officials who wanted to help their people in the four villages that made up the town. Our next step was to invite them all to lunch and explain the work of Light in Africa and the different services that we provide to the community. The Chairman of LIA gave a broad view of our work of caring for the most vulnerable of children. Then, our medical sister explained about the medical work that we do in the remote areas of the bush with our out-reach medical dispensaries provided by our overseas volunteers who fund this vital medical service. Next, our social worker explained the service that she provided to the community, and the government procedures that are required before a child can be accommodated. Lastly, I stood up to speak to the large gathering of people and explained that the reason that we were all here today was because God had sent me to help them. After the hooting and applause had finished, I asked the gathering to tell me what they felt the needs of the community were, and I listened for over an hour to questions and discussions between the leaders. Afterward, everyone shook our hands and welcomed us to contact them if we had any problems. We had formed a plan of action for the way forward, and that was to hold a nine week pilot scheme in the villages with a team of social workers and a medical team, that way we would be able to see the needs of the people.

Tarpaulins had been erected for cover from the sun, and the first of the people in need started to arrive. I was sitting at a desk writing down the usual questions to ask which would then be given to the doctor or the social worker. I was speaking to the Ward Secretary when a man came up to speak to him. He sounded quite secretive as he was whispering. Startled by what the man had whispered, the Ward Secretary just gave me a glancing explanation that this man knew of a disabled child who was locked in a room and left to die by a family member. Five minutes later, he had collected a group of men together and with a "Come. Follow me," I left my chair and just followed the group leaving everyone wondering where I was going.

We reached a house, and there was a lady sitting outside peeling some vegetables. She had a pan of water boiling on three stones. The Ward Secretary spoke to the women, and she refused to answer any of his questions, so the other men tried to encourage her to speak. In the end, the group walked off, and I was just left standing not know-ing what had been said or what had motivated the men to leave. A man's face appeared from behind the house, and he gestured for me to follow him. I walked along the side of the house until I had joined the group where the Ward Secretary was busy hitting a padlock on the outside of the house with a rock. He opened the door, and the men rushed in. The Ward Secretary came to the door and beckoned me inside of the room. My first glance showed me a large piece of plaster that had fallen from the wall and was lying beside a young girl. She was very ridged so I thought perhaps she was suffering from Cerebral Palsy and as she had a spasm she had knocked the plaster off the wall. I knelt down on the floor and took hold of her hand, and she gave me a smile which choked me up. I asked one of the men to gently lift her up and take her outside from the darkened room. The first port of call was the dispensary for the girl of around 11 / 12 years of age to have a full medical before admittance into the care of LIA.

That first pilot scheme day resulted in 140 people being helped and a child's life being saved. After the nine weeks was up, the Executive Management had a meeting to discuss how we could help this impoverished area. The decision was made that, as there were so many vulnerable children roaming the area, we should first consider opening a children's home in this region.

CHAPTER THIRTY-THREE
GOD I NEED AN ANGEL NOW!

With the co-operation of the Ward Secretary of the villages, we managed to find a derelict dispensary with fifteen rooms which required extensive renovation. Our youth Pastor was asked to be the project manager and to move to the area and utilize local builders to build a security wall, have new metal gates welded, and refurbish the rooms.

I received a phone call from the Pastor who gave me a long list of materials that the builders required, so I set off to make the purchases and then deliver them to the property that would be called Fleece House Children's Home.

It wasn't long before I entered the area and became totally lost. It was like a rabbit warren. All around me were houses which had been built of mud bricks and were partially fallen down when the heavy rain hit them. I called Pastor on my mobile, and he asked for me to look a round where I could see any markers. I described a building with an American name and waited patiently until he came into view and drove me to the center. The security wall had not been built as yet, and we drove straight up to the building. As we drove in, I spotted a woman lying flat out on the concrete with a piece of material covering her . "Is she dead?" I asked. Pastor explained that the woman had the HIV/AIDS virus and needed medical care, and with the help of another man, the Pastor had brought the women to wait to see if I would help her by taking her into Moshi to the local government hospital.

I agreed, and she was placed on the back seat of the Serf. A further list of materials was handed to me, and I said I would return as quickly as I could. It took a good couple of hours to pay for the medical bills and doctor's fees before the woman was admitted onto the ward. I then hurriedly drove around buying the rest of the materials required for the dispensary to be changed into a children's home.

It was now getting late, and I decided to grab a quick bite to eat before I travelled over to the mining town again. It had started raining, and I decided to take a guard with me just in case I had a puncture en-route. We set off with the windscreen wipers holding their own until we turned off the tarmac road to go down the road to the mines. I had a whimsical chuckle when I first saw the sign which boasted that a large mining company had made the road and took pride in maintaining it, but it had huge craters embedded in the sand filled road which also had no tarmac, and could cause serious accidents for the many motorbikes which were being used as public transport, especially driving in the dark.

Torrential rain started to pour down, and I was having great difficulty seeing the road as water was streaming across the fields on to the road and over onto the other side. The road looked like a lake. I slowed my pace right down to a crawl as I tried to navigate the road. Just a mile from the dispensary, I hit a large crater, and the car went up to its axle in mud and stopped. I tried to put the car into 4 wheel drive and reverse out of the hole, but all that did was dig me deeper in. I asked the guard to get out of the vehicle, and in driving rain, find me some rocks to put under the rear wheels. He opened the door, and rain lashed at him and drenched him through within seconds of putting his foot in to the hole of water. He held onto the car as he waded to the front of the car and started to bend down to feel for rocks in the water. He had made a couple of journeys to the rear of the vehicle with armful of rocks when, in the cars headlights, I saw him look around. He stood up straight and looked at some approaching lights coming our way. He waited a bit longer looking and listening when he decided to hurry back to the car splashing in the water trying to take large strides. He opened the rear door and dove in. "Look," I said, "We have to have more rocks under the tyre or else we'll never get out of this mess. My phone's dead so I can't ring the pastor to come and help us." As I turned towards the back seat to speak to him, he just pointed to the window with the white of his eyes staring full ahead, said one word, and shot to the floor. "Bandits." My head shot forward towards the front windscreen as I screwed my eyes up to see through the steamed up car window. "Bandits," I responded. As I turned around, six motorcycles started to circle around the car, revving their engines. The full impact of what was about to happen hit me as the motorcycles started to come closer and closer and spray from their motorcycles started to hit the car.

I had heard stories of body parts being sold to the witchdoctors, and as the full enormity of the situation dawned on me that my body parts, because they were white, could possibly be passed off as an albino's. I banged on the steering wheel and screamed in fear, "GOD I NEED AN ANGEL NOW!" The noise of the bikes grew louder as they continued to surround the car. It would just be a matter of time before a rock would be thrown through the window, and I would be pulled out and taken to a certain death. My security guard was useless as he was fumbling under the front passenger seats looking for a weapon or he was trying to hide, I wasn't quite sure which.

In my rear view mirror, I saw headlights approaching coming along the road. The motorcycles must have seen the lights too as they started to withdraw as the vehicle came to a halt. In the headlights of the other vehicle, I watched as the car door opened, and two men in full-length white gowns with a hat on their heads got out of their car. They were joined by two other men who came out of the other side of the door, and they came towards my car. "Oh dear God, help us!" I cried out. My guard was now sitting up and looking out the rear view window, when these four men, who obviously were of the Islam faith, walked at a distance past the car and walked until they were standing in front of my headlights. One of the men shouted, "Mama, you can't stay here. It's too dangerous." Wow, that was an understatement, and how did he know it was me? "Get out of the car and go speak to those men," I instructed my guard. "Look the bikes are over there now." He plodded reluctantly back into the water and the rain. These poor guys were drenched to the skin, and their clothes were stuck to them. "Do you have a tow rope?" the man shouted to me again. Each time I placed my head out of the window, lashing rain hit my face. I shouted to my guard to come back to the car again and take a rope washing line that I had just purchased. He plodded through the lake again and gave it to the man who lifted up his white gown and withdrew a long dagger-shaped knife. He cut the rope twice, and the two of them started to plait the rope. My guard then came and bent down and placed the thin rope through the eye of my car near the bumper. He then went to the back of the car, and the four men got hold of the rope in the front. At his command they all pulled or pushed the car. But nothing happened. They tried again, but the car was stuck and didn't move an inch. The men got in a huddle, and then he shouted to me that they were going to wait for another car to come. He re-iterated to me that I couldn't stay there as it was "too dangerous."

The guard got back into the now soaking wet rear seat, and he asked me if they would leave us. I told him I didn't know. Three of the men got back into the car and one stayed outside. After a little while, lights appeared, and the man started waving his arms in the air. The car came to a halt, and in the still pouring rain, two more gentlemen of the Islam faith came to the front of my vehicle. "Out you get," I said to the guard "and push harder if you want to get home tonight." The rope strained as these 'gifts from God' pulled on the rope and my guard pushed. I felt a slight movement and then another as the car slewed very slowly out of the pot hole and started to slide sideways due to sheer physical strength of the men. I remember a trickle of perspiration dropped from my brow onto my hand as I was clutching the steering wheel so tightly willing the vehicle to move. I started the car and moved the car onto firmer ground. As my wits came back, I thought of how I could reward these extremely kind, brave men who had saved our lives from those bandits who had now left the scene. I fumbled into my purse, and all that I could find having spent the majority of the funds purchasing all the materials was the equivalent to $20.00 I shouted to the guard to come to my window and handed him the money. I shouted a word of thanks to the men who had saved our lives and apologized that I didn't have more money to give them. I was then shocked at what the leader of the group said to me next: "Mama," he shouted back, "we can't take your money as we have just come from the mosque, and Mohammed would not like us to take it. We know of the work that you are doing here, and you are not just here helping the Christian children and adults but also the Muslim, the Hindu's and anyone who needs help, especially the children. We cannot take your money. Use it to buy a soda for the children." And with that they all placed their hands together did a little bow in their fashion, turned away, returned to their car, and I followed their car lights which took me to our center and a warm welcome from our Pastor.

Not only did God answer my urgent request to provide for me one angel, but six came to my rescue.

CHAPTER THIRTY-FOUR
LIFE FOR TUESDAY

Christmas in Tanzania is always quite different from other European countries with the emphasis being firmly placed on the birth of Jesus Christ. The wonderful tolerance and respect that is shown to different faiths is one of the aspects that I just love about this country.

The churches are packed to capacity as believing Christians gather for this very special event in the churches calendar. The shops only start to show Christmas items for sale at the beginning of December unlike their counterparts who often start their commercial campaigns as far back as September. The country is swathed in beautiful red flowers from the Christmas trees (not pine trees) that make the declaration that it is the time of celebration for Christmas, and although we do not actually have any snow with living just 200 kilometers from the equator and the only snow that we see is on the summit of Mount Kilimanjaro, the children's utter joy at receiving a Christmas gift –sometime the very first that they have ever received – makes up for any lost nostalgia about snow for me at Christmas.

If I am speaking at a school engagement overseas just after the Christmas period I will probably ask the children who are seated on the floor this question. "Tell me, What did you get for Christmas?" and hands will excitedly shoot up in the air, every child wanting to tell me what amazing presents that they have received. Some gifts I have never heard of before as technology races forward and leaves me behind in Africa. The answers range from designer clothes, mountain bikes, iPad, and all sorts of different games and gizmos, and then I respond, "How truly amazing all those wonderful gifts that you have received are!" I then ask the children another question: "Would you like to know what my children received for Christmas?" "Yes!" comes back the answer. "Well, my children get so excited when their name is called out, and they come to me to receive their very own plastic bag." A hand will wave in the air with a desperate question to ask. "What's in the plastic bag?" "When they first look inside their bag and find a new toothbrush and toothpaste their joy knows no bounds." The silence is deafening as I wait for the mechanics of their daily lives to absorb the fact that that goes without saying that you have a toothbrush and toothpaste for daily use. Another hand goes up, "Is there anything else in the bag?" "Oh yes, perhaps there will be a small bar of soap, a little toy car for a little boy or a little plastic doll for a little girl, and they all receive a packet of sweets, or crayons and a colouring book, and perhaps some new underwear and socks for school. All the children are just so overjoyed with their gifts, because for some of these children, it is the very first time that they have ever received a gift just for themselves to keep. The children are all dressed on Christmas day in their new second-hand clothes that we have bought specially for them from the local market, so when we all come together for our celebration of the birth of Jesus the children are all happy and joyful wearing their new clothes. We have a great time together, and this is followed by our Christmas lunch. We are one big happy family. Even though there are over 250 children in our family so we really know how to have a good party.

A lot of discussion ensues from this picture of an African Christmas.

One of the rules that we live by is: if we can't afford it, we don't buy it. We have our priorities whenever we receive any funding or donations. First, we purchase food and, if possible, fill our silos up with maize and beans in case there is a drought. Secondly, medical expenses are taken care of, as we have a lot of sick children in our care (we have children with the HIV/AIDS virus besides the 'special needs' facility). Education comes third in line with, school fees accounting for over $52,000 per year from our yearly budget with over 200 children attending school to ensure the children are well educated. Lastly, we pay staff wages/utilities and running expenses. We have no debt, or bank loans, and if our purse is empty, it's only because God is going to fill it up again. I have a saying that is rather like a mantra: "God cannot re-fill a full purse, so the purse has to be emptied to allow Him to refill it."

The wonderful volunteers who deem to join us to help prepare for the Christmas spirit usually start to arrive around the 16th of December, and they immediately become heavily involved in our preparations. Can you imagine it? We purchase a new set of second-hand clothes for every child, ensuring the list is checked and re-checked for the Christmas presents. We also ensure all the gifts from the overseas sponsors are given to the child and thank you letters written back, and make sure all the food for three days of celebrations is enough to feed everyone, including a further 300 children at the Food Kitchen at the mining town.

Boxing day finds our volunteers and staff bumping down the road in our thirty year old Land Rover to distribute 600 "Christmas Crackers" which are filled with two large exercise books, two pens, two pencils, an eraser, and a pencil sharpener then topped off with sweets and rolled up to look like a cracker. In Tanzania, if you have no uniform or school materials then the teacher will turn you away from school, as she probably is teaching a class of 70 to 120 children in one class and will look for any opportunity to reduce her class size. Each year, we follow the same pattern on Boxing Day. First, we distribute the 'crackers' to a very poor Maasai school where the children have no desks and sit on the mud floor, and then we go to the Food Kitchen for their Christmas party and their gift of a 'cracker.' Two years ago, a turn of events would see me two weeks later at a private hospital in Nairobi, Kenya.

We had clapped our hands in sheer delight when the young primary school Maasai children had sang songs for their guests in English, and we had joined in with the 'action' songs, then it was time for all of the children to line up and receive their Christmas Cracker. As the children eagerly opened the crackers to get at the sweets, a Maasai woman whom I knew came up to me and took my hand and started to drag me away from the school.

Eight months earlier, I had been asked by a local village leader if I would help some very young Maasai children whom had been left behind with extended family members or neighbours whilst their parents, babies on the breast, and older children, walked over 200 kilometers to the grass lands. Their cattle already looked like clothes racks with their bones sticking out, and it would only be a matter of time before the animals would not have sufficient energy to walk the distance and would die en-route. As the families who were deemed to care for these young children, who were too young to walk with their parents, had very little food for their own children due to the drought, these little ones were going very hungry and were hanging around the school in the hope someone would give them some food. Whenever I receive a referral for assistance, I never take anything at face value and always investigate each request for myself, and what I found in this instance was very young children, eighteen months and over, with their young bodies already showing signs of malnutrition.

After we had opened our first children's home at the mining area, children living on the streets were coming to the gate and asking for food. We made the decision that we had to support these children if they were to survive, and so we opened our five day a week Food Kitchen which provides a nourishing meal with vegetables and a piece of fruit and a cup of clean water, as all the water in the area has a high fluoride content and distorts soft bones. We purchase water each day which has been transported in from the main line 20 kilometers away. Since the opening of the Food Kitchen, well over 520,000 meals had been served to these most vulnerable of children.

For our Food Kitchen cooks, it would mean extra preparation of two more huge pans which have the capacity to feed 100 children per pan.

Each day, with additional barrels of clean water, spinach, and a piece of fresh fruit, the little toddlers would first wash their hands, and then wait patiently in line until it was their turn to collect a plate of food and a cup of clean drinking water. What always amazed our volunteers or visitors who were accompanying me to the school was the fact that all of these children, including the children attending the school, would take their plates and drinks into the classroom, sit down on the mud floor and wait patiently until all the children had received their plate of food and grace for the food had been said. Even though they were so hungry, they would wait, and then after the grace, they would dig in lick the plates clean, and look for any 'seconds' that may be had.

This extra food kitchen at the school had continued until the Maasai returned to their encampments when the rains came and the grass grew back again sufficiently for the cows to eat.

As the Maasai mama pulled me away from the group, I thought she was going to ask me about her baby son whom I had taken into care some month's earlier when the famine was at its height.

I had been packing away the empty pill bottles after we had just held an out-reach medical dispensary when this Maasai mama came and placed a baby in my arms. As I looked at its matchstick arms and legs, I said to the mama, "If you don't allow me to take this baby now into LIA home, you will be burying the boy within a few days. Go now, to your husband and village leaders and tell them what I want to do." She left me holding the baby whilst she completed the necessary requirements for me to bring the baby into care. I explained that the child was so severely malnourished I could not make any guarantee's that it would survive, but with God's help and prayers, we would do our very best. The poor women had no breast milk, and she herself was in a terribly neglected state, so I arrange for a sack of maize out of our store to be delivered to her to feed her other children. As she is literally dragging me by my hand to accompany her this Boxing Day, I shouted to the volunteers to follow me to her boma (round house made of sticks and cow dung). When we arrived outside her boma, she quickly shouted to her neighbours to bring for her "honoured guests" something for them to sit on. Rocks, empty oil drums, and a small three legged milking stool were quickly found, and we were summoned to sit. When we were all seated to her satisfaction, she went inside her boma and brought out a child of around seven years of age and stood him directly in front of me. There were gasps from the volunteers as this little boy stood looking at me, and I could see he was a very sick child. His lymph nodes down each side of his neck were badly swollen and running with puss. I looked at the mother who dashed into her boma again and this time returned with a letter which she thrust into my hands. The letter was written in English and from a local hospital which diagnosed that this child was suffering from cancer leukemia, and the only course of action would be for the child to go to a hospital 500 kilometers away for chemotherapy treatment. The volunteers wanted to know what the letter said, and I repeated the diagnosis. Tony, a businessman from America, who is a regular visitor to LIA each Christmastime, was emphatic that I should help this child. The letter that I held in my hand was dated over a year ago. Many questions were asked of the mother until I could make sense of it all. Apparently the child had become sick, had visited two hospitals, spending three months in one of them before the diagnosis was given of Leukemia.

The boy's father owned only one cow which he had sold to pay for the hospital bill, but had no money left for any further treatment. The child had stayed in the mud hut for the last twelve months with not even a pain relief tablet. It was pretty evident that Tony was getting very emotional about the suffering of this child and he was quite insistent that I should "do something to help him." "Of course I will help him Tony, but I will not take this child for chemotherapy treatment 500 kilometers away. I will not put this child through that. I will however, take care of him and keep him as 'pain free' until he passes over. But in the mean time, we are all going to get into the vehicle and go see the doctor I work with here for his medical opinion."

We all piled into the vehicle and mindful that all the children at the Food Kitchen would be waiting patiently for our arrival to start the party, we headed off to visit the dispensary where my two dear doctor friends whom we have worked with and supported for quite some time would be able to advise me as to the way forward to help this child.

We were welcomed by the doctor, and after all the greetings and book signings were completed, the doctor stood the child in front of him and silently prayed for the child before he placed his stethoscope in his ears to listen to the child's chest. After looking at all of his lymph nodes, he said, "You do know that this child is very sick don't you?" "Yes, I do," I responded and handed him the letter from the hospital to read. After reading the letter, he examined the child named Tuesday – because his mother had given birth to him on a Tuesday – again and said, "You know the hospital is recommending Chemotherapy?" "Yes, I know that, too, but for me that isn't in the equation. I cannot hold this boy's hand whilst he undergoes such invasive treatment. I just can't and won't do it." At this remark, Tony became extremely upset, either with me or the situation, I wasn't quite sure which. I sat back in the chair and waited for the doctor to complete his examination. Quite suddenly, an idea sprang into my mind, a kind of spiritual awakening. "Tony," I said, "are you prepared to help this boy if I take him to a private hospital in Kenya?" Where this idea materialized from, I had no idea because I had never been to Nairobi in Kenya before. He quickly responded and said he would donate $500.00. "Right, I will leave the earliest I can when I have all the Immigration paperwork completed for the boy and his mother to travel with me. The only real problem that I see is that I don't speak Kiswahili or Maasai, so I guess I will go back to my old profession of signing and miming to make myself understood. We returned the child and his mother back to their boma with some pain relief medication for Tuesday and then drove off to the Food Kitchen party.

We arrived in Nairobi on a Sunday, and I booked the three of us into a cheap hotel. The following morning, we took a taxi to a private hospital, not knowing what the outcome of this impulsive decision that I had made would lead us. We were shown into a room to meet with a pediatrician who required Tuesday to undergo many tests to enable her to get a clear diagnoses after reading the referral letter from the hospital in Tanzania which clearly stated that Tuesday was suffering from Leukemia.

By 4:00 p.m. in the afternoon of my first day, I had spent $300.00, and I was starting to become a little anxious of the 'money situation', and now the pediatrician was asking for me to go to the Pathology department to have a blood draw. "How much is this going to cost," I thought as I headed to the cashiers department to pay for the test. We were then directed to go to the other side of the hospital, and as we were walking down this long corridor, I inadvertently bumped into someone whilst trying to explain to the mother what was now going to happen to Tuesday, "Oh" I am so terribly sorry," I said, apologetically to the well-dressed lady that I had bumped into. "It is my fault entirely I do apologize." She raised her hands and said, "No matter. Are you looking for somewhere?" "Yes," I responded. "I'm trying to find the Pathology department." "I can help you," she said. "That's my department," and we started to walk down the corridor together. She then asked me what I was doing with a Maasai mama and a child, and I told her the whole story of how we had found the child in a mud hut where he had been over a year with no medication with a diagnosis of cancer. We arrived at her department, and whilst she called a technician to take Tuesday for his blood draw, the pathologist asked me to tell her more about the work of Light in Africa. On 'Tuesday's return, I shook hands with this most gracious of ladies, and she asked me to return early the following morning to collect the results for me to be able to give them to the pediatrician.

When we arrived at the Pathology department the following morning, the lady was waiting for our arrival. She handed me the brown envelope with the results in and then made a startling statement.

She said, "I couldn't get this little boy out of my mind, and last night, I explained the situation to my husband who is also a doctor, and we both prayed for the child. (When she made this statement that she and her husband had prayed for Tuesday, flashlights went off in my head, and I knew without a shadow of doubt, God was in this situation and that He had a plan.) "What I would like to do," she continued, "is to extract some contents from his face and grow a culture to gain it's DNA, and then I will know for sure if it is cancer or not." She wanted to know if I would be prepared to hold the boy down whilst she did this procedure. She stated that he would be given a sedative that would not anaesthetize him, just make him a little sleepy and relax him. I thanked this Christian woman profusely, and left to give the blood test results to the pediatrician.

That afternoon Tuesday was given a sedative, but he knew something was going down and every time the curtain around the bed was drawn, he would sit up in bed expectantly. We waited a good thirty minutes, but there was no way he was going to sleep so with a technician holding his feet, and me holding his face completely still, the doctor extracted four phials of "gunk" from his cheeks. The Pathologist then told me I would have to wait three or four days for the result to be confirmed. I said I had to leave Kenya on Friday morning as all my money would be gone by then. She replied that she would do her very best, and I knew that she would. Thursday night at 7:00 p.m., my mobile phone rang. "Mama Tuesday," the voice said, "come to the Pathology department and collect the envelope that is waiting for you on the desk," and with that comment the phone cut off. "That sounded very ominous," I thought, and I called for a taxi to take me to the hospital. I walked down the long corridor and spoke to the technician on night duty, telling her that I had come to collect an envelope from the Pathologist's desk. She handed me the brown envelope, and

I prayed for the child before I opened it, fully aware what the implications for this child could be. I had grown quite fond of Tuesday over these last few days, and it was lovely to see him smile and laugh as he tried out new foods like beef burgers and chips and sodas. Whilst his mother kept to a diet of rice or ugali, he was daring enough to experiment with different foods instead of the traditional flour and water diet of ugali and beans. Whilst at the hostel, he had suffered a really severe nose bleed, and he had just been so brave whilst I followed the usual procedures to stop the flow, and I wondered if nose bleeds was going to part of his on-going condition.

I slowly opened the envelope and removed the letter from inside.

My eye's scrolled down all the headings, and stopped and stared at the sentence that declared NO CANCER FOUND.

With an abundance of drugs for his 'massive' infection, we returned home.

Tuesday and his younger brother still live in the care of Light in Africa and are doing extremely well.

Tony, our volunteer who was persistently insistent that I help the child, was so delighted with Tuesday's recovery that he always makes a 'bee line' to see him when he arrives to help us at Christmas. We give God the Glory, and we bless all the people involved in Tuesday's incredible recovery.

CHAPTER THIRTY-FIVE
BREATHE ON HER
BREATH OF GOD

How little the rich man knows,

Of what the poor man feels,

When want, like some dark demon foe,

Nearer and nearer steals.

He never saw his darlings lie,

Shivering on flags their bed,

He never heard that maddening cry

"Daddy a bit more bread."

Ist & 4ᵗʰ verse from Mary Barton Chapter 6 By Elizabeth Gaskell.

Each year, we receive at Light in Africa many returning overseas volunteers who have previously stayed with our mission and visited again either to work their internship with us in social work or in the medical field, working in local hospitals, on outreach dispensary programmes, or just returning each year at Christmas time to enjoy all the festivities and see the children so happy with their small gift that they receive.

Tom was one such young man who first volunteered with his medical university student group, and they raised much needed funds by cycling the length of the British Isles from Lands' End to John o' Grouts which is from the tip to the bottom of the UK consisting of approx. 1,000 miles or 1600 km. Tom returned the following year as a coordinator for Light in Africa and for the many volunteers who arrive during the months of June/July/August ensuring that they all settle in well into their accommodation, know the 'do's and the 'don'ts and everyone was well supported. He was able to answer the many questions about the Tanzanian culture from asking if they were inappropriately dressed, to what should they expect to experience on the Maasai four day walk into the bush and are they likely to encounter any wild animals. Every question asked receives a truthful answer.

Tom had accompanied me out to the mining town where Light in Africa had established two children's homes plus the food kitchen. Whilst we stood around chatting with the doctor, suddenly a thin, 6' tall maasai warrior rushed past us into the doctors' room carrying an unconscious child in his arms.

A few minutes later, the doctor came to his surgery door and called for me to come into his office. I hurried into his room followed by Tom. "Mama Lynn, will you help this Maasai? He has no money and his niece is going to die unless she gets to the hospital in time. She has eaten a yellow highly toxic plant with a hard shell which has lodged in her windpipe and is stopping the flow of oxygen. If the shell of the plant breaks the toxins will kill her. It can and does kill cows. "Yes, of course I will," I replied automatically, "How long do you think we have to get her to the hospital? She is becoming very weak." "About forty minutes before her organs start to collapse," he replied. "That's not possible," I responded tensely, "as it will take us at least fifty five minutes to get to casualty." He could see my concern as I shouted to our driver to start the car, and I turned and asked Tom if he would accompany me to the hospital. He agreed, and we both got into the back seat of the car with the child's uncle sitting next to the driver.

The doctor laid the child, who was still unconscious, on our laps with me cradling the child's head backwards to try to allow as much oxygen into her lungs as possible. The doctor gave a demonstration to Tom on how to give her cardiac massage and with a fleeting "May God be with you," the vehicle moved off onto the pot-holed sand road where there was not an inch of tarmac laid.

The LIA driver put the head lamps on full beam and started blowing his horn to try to move the herd of donkeys carrying water containers out of his way as we raced along these dangerous roads which the miners use.

I held the child's head tightly to try to stop the neck from breaking as we sprung into the air over road bumps and landed heavily, while Tom was trying to keep a rhythm going with his fingertips, and the perspiration was already collecting on his face due to the heat and the concentration. We reached the main road, and the driver increased the vehicle's speed, as he weaved past cars and police check points with his lights on and horn blaring. I admired once again our drivers' commitment to our children, for when push comes to shove, their very best is revealed. A change occurred in the child's face, and I knew she was dying. "Quick, Tom. Hit her harder," I yelled above the noise of the engine. He made his fingertips, which must have been aching by this point, into a fist and hit her chest. She rallied around and opened her eyes for a short time, then they rolled back into her head. "Tom! Hit her again," I shouted desperately, and once again, he thumped down hard on her chest. The words of an old hymn started playing in my mind, "Breath on me, breath of God, and fill me with life anew." As I was already praying in the Spirit, I decided to change the words of the hymn and started, in my mind praying, 'breath on her, breath of God, and fill her with life anew.' Tom thumped on her heart again, and at this point I could not see the child hanging on much longer. Obviously the obstruction was blocking the airway and her organs were having to work twice as hard, but now they were very weak and about to collapse.

We screeched to a halt at the doorway to casualty, and Tom ran her into an anti-room and laid her on a table, still unconscious.

I turned my back from where the seven year old was lying as a doctor came through the door and approached me. "What's the problem?" he asked. I relayed the events to him and asked him to speak to the uncle if he required further details. Just then I felt a movement on my back, and wondered what it was. I spun around to see Sophia sitting up on the bed trying to cover her exposed legs with her shuka (material). Wide-eyed and in total disbelief, I looked to Tom for an explanation, and he replied that as soon as the nurse placed the oxygen pipes into her nostril she came around straight away and sat up. The hymn that I had been singing in my spirit came into my mind. "Breath on her, breath of God, and fill her with life anew," Edwin Hatch's (1835-1889) hymn that he wrote which I had sung many times growing up and attending churches and chapels and was a great favourite of my mother's.

Breathe on me, breath of God;

Fill me with life anew,

That I may love what thou dost love;

And do what thou wouldst do.

Sophia was rushed to theatre and the offending toxic ball was removed. If at any time it had burst whilst the doctors where extracting it, there was no doubt in anyone's mind that the child would have died.

Whilst waiting for Sophia to be returned to the ward, I asked the uncle why had the child eaten this toxic plant which was full of poison when I knew full well that a young Maasai girl from an early age would have been involved in cattle herding for the family, and she would have been taught to keep the animals away from the plant that could kill it, so why had she eaten it! The uncle replied, "We had no food to eat at home last night or this morning due to the drought, so when she asked me for food this morning I told her to go look in the fields for something to eat. I knew that there was nothing there, but I just wanted to get her out of my way. That is why she tried to eat the plant because she was so hungry."

On my return to the mining town, I arranged for sacks of maize to be carried on two donkeys into the uncle's settlement as there were also nine other children suffering without food.

Incidents like this happen when there is no rainfall to grow the maize, and it dies on the stalk. This is abstract poverty where children die of hunger.

CHAPTER THIRTY-SIX
THE WITCHDOCTORS REWARD

(Do not read this true article if you are of a sensitive disposition.)

It was going to be another scorching hot day in Tanzania, as the group of volunteers hauled all the trunks full of medical supplies in to the back of the Land Rover. We could already feel the African sun beating down upon our backs, and we ensured we had plenty of bottled water with us to quench our thirst during the long day. No food was allowed to be taken on these medical outreaches for fear of hand to mouth transmissions. Bottled water only was the order of the day. Our doctor was meticulously checking everything in to the vehicle as we could not afford to leave anything behind today because we were going deep into the bush.

All checks completed, we climbed in to the vehicle, with the medical staff taking the front seats in order to show the driver where our dispensary was to be held on this occasion. The enthusiastic volunteers full of expectations were chatting non-stop in the rear of the vehicle. I smiled to myself as I knew this would be a very different story on the return journey. They would be too exhausted to even grunt after seeing anything from two to three hundred patients today. Bush telegraph had been passed around for around three weeks telling of our dispensary date, and people would walk for miles around to come to see the doctor.

A queue had already gathered as the driver searched for a large tree with overhanging branches under which to park the vehicle just to try to glean some shade from the intense heat.

For the poor of this area, this dispensary would be there only life-line to any form of 'free' medical assistance or in any eventuality of them requiring surgery to have Light in Africa pay for their hospital medical bills.

Normally, if you are poor and have no money, then you don't even try to access any form of medical help. First, you would have to have money to travel to a dispensary, then you would then require money to open a file, money again to see the doctor, money for any tests that the doctor would advise, money again for any medicines the doctor would recommend. So if you have no money, you either hope to get better, or take traditional medicines, or worse, you die.

With our unique volunteer program where we ask volunteers to raise sufficient funds to help our children or the community, the vol-unteers themselves make the decision as to where these funds will be spent. They have complete control over the funds that they have raised, allowing for full transparency, whereby the volunteer's donors can see photo's of the projects and the receipts to ensure full account-ability.

Medical students and electives from overseas particularly enjoy this opportunity to see medical conditions which developed countries have already eradicated. Our local medical doctor has been named by our volunteers 'the happiest man on the planet' – as he has such an enigmatic disposition and is always smiling and willing to explain conditions in depth to our medical students, even though he may have a couple of hundred people waiting for him to diagnose their conditions. He truly has the patience of Job, and is a great favourite among the volunteers.

The doctor went straight to his makeshift room to prepare for his first patient. Tables were set up for the nurse, to enable her to dispense the medication, and the volunteers where helping to place pills in plastic bags. Stacks of anti-malaria drugs, medicines for respiratory tract infections, and eye drops for the many eye conditions that they would see today due to the dust in the environment. Everything was now ready to start the dispensary.

My table was close to the door to enable me to 'queue manage' all these people, and my colleague would take registration and complete the usual personal history prior to seeing the doctor.

I would also be on the 'look-out' for any child that had head fungi which would mean a head wash and cream applied by a volunteer. If this condition went untreated, the whole household would be infected, and as most families all slept in one bed in a small bedroom, the chances of transmission were very high. Just before I sat at the table to start the procession of patients, I took a long drink of water, and as I screwed on the bottle top, I looked along the line of waiting patients, and that's when I saw her for the first time. You couldn't miss her. She stuck out like a very sore thumb. A white Albino child held tightly by an elderly lady. I knew instinctively why she was here today. The small child was squirming to try to gain her freedom. I surmised it could be her grandmother who was holding her in a vice-like grip. I started to move the patients to various stations. Twenty patients would have to be seen before it would be the turn of the grandmother.

The national and local newspapers were full of the atrocities that were occurring throughout the whole of Tanzania, and especially in the lakes area, where groups of men – on demand from the witchdoctors - would capture albino children on their way to school, or adults, and kill them for their body parts, which when dissected, brought in large amounts of money for the dealers in albino deaths. It only took the suggestion by the witchdoctors that great wealth and prosperity would be gained for anyone who owned a piece of albino, and the grizzly trade had begun.

The Tanzanian Government had promising the 'wananchi' (people) that the perpetrators would be severely punished for these heinous crimes.

LIA already was caring for a number of albino children, who had sad stories to tell of stones being thrown at them and taunted by local children, their parents afraid to let them out of their sight, and many were kept locked away in rooms for their own safety. Albino's also had many medically issues, some of which were poor eyesight, heart problems, and skin conditions, which meant that they could not go out into the sun without using skin moisturizer and wearing protective clothing, for fear of cancer. But the deepest pain, I sense, is from their own people, who have ostracized, and marginalized this minority group.

As the grandmother and child moved towards our desk for registration, they had been joined by a younger lady, whom I assumed was the child's mother. Before we had even written down their names, the mother was on her knees, with her hands clasped, crying out to God for the 'wazungu' to take her child. I helped the woman up from her knees, and both the women were now openly crying and beseeching me to take the child into care. We were now joined by other patients who were offering support to the distressed mother.

I asked my colleague, to go and fetch the doctor. He came over and took the mama and the grandmother over into his room, whilst I gave the little girl a sweet, and moved her away from the crowds. I estimated the child was about three years of age, with very fair skin. As I gave her a wrapped sweet, she held it up very close to her eyes to see whether it really was a sweet, and her eyesight appeared to be very poor. Being satisfied that it was indeed a sweet, she opened it and ate it.

I left her with a volunteer, and went into the doctor's office to find out the facts. The mother was still weeping, and when I walked in, she got up from her chair, held onto me, and cried, and cried. She was about to give her daughter to someone else to be looked after, and it was causing her, quite naturally, deep emotional pain. The story the grandmother told the doctor was that the mother and grandmother were finding it difficult to live, as they couldn't go out and look for work. One of them had to remain in their home, locked in with the child. They had been told by neighbours that a reward was being offered by the witchdoctor's that said they would pay $4,000 to anyone who would abduct the child and bring her to them. They feared it was only a matter of time before the mob broke into their home and abducted the child.

The following day, with high security, we took the child by Land Rover to a place of safety. As the child sat on my knee, she kept repeating the same words over and over again. "Naogopa, naogopa," which, when translated, means, "I'm scared, I'm worried." Little did this little one know, that her life had just drastically changed for the better, and that now in the care of LIA, every opportunity to enhance her life would be given to her. She is now receiving an education in a secure school.

CHAPTER THIRTY-SEVEN
CHOLERA STRIKES

Word quickly spread, like a California fire, that cholera had hit the mining town. As more cases were identified on a daily basis, it wasn't long before the army was called in to ensure all necessary health controls were being adhered to and local leaders were implementing the 'shut down' of road side businesses selling food, sometimes the only way that women with families had the ability to feed their children. It was a desperate time, and consequently at our children's home within the area, it was also a 'no one in – no one out' situation. Weekly food had to be taken to the door of the children's home and left outside. This reminded me very much of how the plaque which struck the UK must have placed fear in the hearts of many people. One dispensary was identified as the place that all cholera victims were referred for medical attention. It was the doctor that we used when our children from the children's home were sick. We found him to be a very sensitive and humble man, who had great compassion for his patients, and in an emergency situation, he would often ring and ask for our help in taking a patient to the nearest hospital which was quite a drive away. I well remember sitting in the doctor's surgery one day discussing a particular case, when we heard a child screaming some distance away, and as the distressed child came closer the screaming became intense. The doctor jumped up from his chair when the child was seen through his window, and was brought into his surgery. He immediately asked for me to take the child, who had no skin on her torso from the waist upwards, to hospital. Whilst my driver exceeded the speed limit, I was sitting on the back seat trying to stop the child's mother, who was insisting on putting a dirty piece of material over the burn to cover the child up, which resulted in further screams from the child as the material touched her raw skin.

Three hours later, the child at last receives a pethidine injection, and the screaming stopped. My nerves were absolutely jangled, and on the return journey, I couldn't close my mind to the child's screams.

But now it was how to keep everyone safe in the homes.

I had returned to our headquarters at Mailisita, when, at 7am one morning, I receive a telephone call from the doctor. "Mama please can you help me? I have eight new cholera patients, and I have used all of my own money on drugs. I need ten bottles of fluids per patient plus candelas. Do you have any means to help me?" Quickly calculating, that meant he would require eighty bottles of fluid. I knew we had no such amount as this in our own dispensary, only drugs and dressings. "I'll ring you back when I have consulted with our midwife," I said, knowing full well what she would say. I said a quick arrow prayer, something like, "Dear God, you know the need of these desperately sick people, and the desperation of this doctor who is totally exhausted from all this devastating outbreak. Please find a way for me to help him, and bring an end to this dreadful disease." I walked out of my room and started to walk down the corridor to the stairs. As I started to descend, I noticed a tall, middle-aged man, following my movements. Walking outside, the man walked forward and introduced himself as Anton from Germany, and he had heard about the works of LIA and decided to visit us the next time he was in Tanzania. As we stood chatting, our midwife who cares for the children in our home's came into view. "Excuse me please, Anton I have an urgent request to attend to. Can you tell me please sister? Do we have any fluids or candela at the dispensary?" "No. Nothing. Why?" she asked, and I relayed the doctors story of eight new cases. "Can I help?" this gentlemen asked. "Do you have funds to purchase eighty bottles of fluid?" I offered. "Yes, I do," he responded. "Will you go with sister and purchase the fluids which might save the lives of these cholera victims?" I asked. "Yes. On one condition," he replied. "And what is that condition?" I asked hesitantly. "That I can go and deliver the bottles with the sister to the dispensary." "You can on my condition," I responded, "and that is you do not get out of the vehicle. You must stay inside the vehicle, we cannot risk you touching anything. We will just blow the car horn and leave the area. If you promise to do that, it will be ok." He agreed, and they both left to purchase the drugs and make the delivery.

At eight in the evening, I hear a text message being delivered to my mobile phone. It read: "All patients recovering. Praise the Lord."

These victims were the last patients to be found with the disease.

CHAPTER THIRTY-EIGHT
AHSANTE SANA MAMA

From day to day I never know where I shall be sleeping that night.

It could be at any one of our children's homes, in any one of their bedrooms, especially if there is a staff shortage or a particular problem arises. Or I could stay the night, when a room is available, at Tudor Village in one of TorchBearer's quality accommodations where I can access a hot shower unlike when I stay in the homes. For instance, as I write, I'm living with our older girls in their home called Newcastle House (because the volunteers from Newcastle University-UK built it over a two year period) and as the water supply is such a problem here with over 100 girls living on the site, each evening I fill two 1 1/2 litre bottles and my little red bucket with water. I do this because, sometimes in the morning, you can prepare to take your shower and get all soaped up and then someone turns on an outside tap, - usually the kitchen — and then there is no more water. At this point, you're left standing there until they switch the tap off again, so I have learnt from past experience what a good idea it is to have some bottled water handy to wash the soap suds off.

When I lived at the White House, Mailisita, in one year I moved fourteen times from bedroom to bedroom as the need for the bedroom that I was staying in became apparent that it was needed. This is not perhaps a particular lifestyle that the average person would like to swap with me, as people tend to like their many home comforts. I don't have any.

At the mining town, we operate two children's homes and a food kitchen from three different facilities. I spent a year living in this town before my health deteriorated with all of the dust that is floating about in the air. The area, which has no banks, –because of the criminal activity there, they - would be robbed – no post offices, or even a bakery. The mining town was a really desperate environment to live in with many different tribes coming together with one purpose only in mind, to dig for gemstones.

Late one evening, our staff manager answered a hard knock on the security gate. She peeped through the little opening which allowed her to see who was standing there without opening the gate. Mary, our truly dedicated Fleece House manager, recognized a local village leader whom she knew, and she opened the security gate for him to enter along with other visitors.

The Leader was accompanied by the relative of a little boy of around five years of age whom the manager noticed was in such a pitiful state of weakness and badly injured, that she immediately called our other staff members to come to her assistance to help the child.

Mary was to hear from the Leader of the village one of the most cruel, brutal cases of child abuse that she had ever heard.

The boy's father was a miner, and he lived with his son whom he named after the disciple who betrayed Jesus. One day, he came home and severely beat the child with a stick and padlocked him in his hut and left him inside for three days with no food. The boy's relative, who knew what had happened, and where culture demanded she did not interfere, could stand it no longer and reported the case to the Leader of the village. The boy was released from his prison and both of them had brought the injured child straight to Light in Africa.

Now one of the things that everyone knows about Mary is that you don't mess with her, and she took immediate control of the situation.

"First, she informed the Leader and the relative to go and report this abuse to the local police station, receive a PO3 for a medical examination, and have the father arrested immediately. "Secondly," she said, "I am not going to receive this child into LIA care unless I have a detailed medical report from a medical practitioner of every single beat mark and bump on this poor child's body. With the state he is in, he could die from internal injuries. Only when these two instructions have been dealt with will I receive the child into full-time care."

The child had been so badly beaten around his waist and his back that he could hardly move without feeling intense pain. Over the following weeks, he never spoke one word, he was so badly traumatized. Each day a carer would gently 'bed bath' him and then carry him to a soft padded cushion which was placed outside the kitchen door. There he would receive a plate of food that was placed between his legs, and over a two hour period, he would try to slowly eat the food whilst he watched our other children playing.

Five weeks later, I am busy in the office of Fleece House updating files and writing reports when I opened the bottom drawer of a filing cabinet and find a large packet of sweet lollipops. I walked to the door of the office, and holding up the bag of lollipops, I shouted to all of the children playing around, "moja moja" (one by one). Seeing the bag of sweets the children immediately stopped playing their games and ran to get into line. As they all shuffled to get into position, with the older girls placing the smaller children to the front of the line, I said, "Look what I have found! Have you all been good children today?" Nods of agreement with big smiles on their faces and hand waving were their response. All eyes were on the bag of sweets as I pulled the bag open to reveal the lollipops. It was then as I stood on the steps that I saw Steven, who was sat on his cushion watching the children since his arrival at the home, start to carefully place his elbows on to the wall behind him in an endeavor to raise himself to a standing position. As I stared at this little scrap of humanity trying to raise himself to his feet, all the children in the line followed my gaze to watch Steven do something he had never done before. He shakily stood a moment to gain his balance, and then when he felt he was sufficiently stable he placed his first foot forward, and with hunched shoulders and head down, he very very slowly started to walk towards the line of children. When Steven eventually reached the line, children moved either forward or backwards to allow him to stand in the line along with them. Emotionally choked up at what I had just witnessed, I started to give the lollipops out to the little tots at the front of the line, and each child either gave me a little nod of the head or a little curtsy and said, 'Ahsante Sana mama' (thank you mama). The children peeled away and moved over to the litter bin to place their wrappers from the lollipops into the bin. It was now Stevens turn to receive his lollipop and still with his head down, he held out his hand to receive the sweet, and in a whispered voice said, 'Ahsante Sana mama.' These were the first words that the child had uttered in five weeks.

Eight months later, I am enjoying a mug of tea and looking out of the window watching the children playing whilst I waited for my transport to arrive from the filling station when I put my mug down on my desk to peer more intently out of the window. "What's he up to?" I thought as I watched Steven on his tip toes sneaking up to a group of his friends. Measuring in his mind the distance he would have to run, he reached out and pinched one of the boys on his bum. Of course this brought an immediate reaction as the boy chased him around the playground. And there Steven was giggling and laughing.

CHAPTER THIRTY-NINE
TUDOR VILLAGE - OUR OWN PLACE AT LAST

With just two years left to run on our lease at the white house, the Executive Committee of LIA decided that we should start to pray for our own land and move there when the lease was completed.

Prayers being answered and with grateful thanks to our wonderful friends in Malibu, California, we were able to purchase a fourteen acre site at Bomang'ombe close to the Kilimanjaro International Airport with the Sanya Juu river running past the land. We would then be able to utilize the river water to irrigate our crops, which in turn would help us to become more self-sustainable with growing as much of our own food as we could to help feed the children. I called the site Tudor Village as I could see the country of Tanzania was starting to change its focus. Mobile phones and computers were being imported, and a shift in consciousness was taking place. I recalled during the Tudor period in England, innovation of new exciting ideas took place as ships started to travel to find 'new worlds'. With the help of our volunteers and legacies, we started to build our quality Tudor homes which would become the home for our girls.

Since we left the White House and moved to the site, development has been outstanding and we now have a beautiful environment which houses six homes, including a 'special need's unit, a community center, and a Torchbearers Family Business for our children to learn life-skills which was built for tourist and guest accommodations in Tudor Houses and Makuti Lodges.

CHAPTER FORTY
IN THE MOMENT

I had agreed with my son Marcus that I would be waiting at the junction of the main road from the Kilimanjaro International Airport, and he would, after completing the daily school run, collect the volunteers from Tudor Village. He would then pick me up, and we would continue the drive to Arusha, which was a further 60 kilometers away. I had been waiting a good thirty minutes in the warmth of the morning sun and taking in the Maasai in their brightly coloured reds and blue shukas as they herded their goats to a parking lot for a lorry to arrive and purchase the goats from them. I said a little arrow prayer for the goats as I knew they were being bought for slaughter.

I then spotted Light in Africa's mini-bus coming down the road. Marcus brought the vehicle to a stop beside me and started to apologize for being late, saying nothing had gone right for him that morning. The children whom he picked up every day to take to school had not been ready, and he had to wait for them, and he had failed to collect the volunteers so we would have to turn around and go pick them up first before starting our journey to Arusha.

I climbed into the front passenger seat of the vehicle, and we set off. As I started to buckle my seat belt into its holster, I suddenly asked my son a question... "Do we have a First Aid Kit in the car?" Without verbally responding, he pulled up the compartment between us, and I could see through the plastic First Aid bag the items that lie inside. He replaced the cover and carried on driving down the road. About three minutes later, we rounded a corner and immediately came upon a road traffic accident.

Vehicles had stopped in front of us, and many people were milling around. We slowed down, and we saw in a field a vehicle sitting on its roof. I suggested to Marcus that as there were a lot of people available to help, he should try to get passed the parked lorry which was straddling the road. A group of people spotted LIA's vehicle and came running over to us and started banging on the side panels asking us to stop the vehicle.

"Pull over, Marcus," I said somewhat reluctantly. "I guess we're needed.' I'll take the First Aid Kit and go sit on the back seat. There's no police or ambulance here yet, so you go see who we can help." I alighted from the front seat, slid the side door open, and climbed onto the back seat. As I retrieved a pair of latex gloves from the First Aid Kit, I looked out of the window and saw four men hurrying towards the vehicle each holding onto an arm or a leg of a man who they were carrying with his face to the ground. When they reached our vehicle, a woman got into the vehicle sitting beside me, and the men then laid this bleeding man across our laps.

Marcus was walking a lady by the arm, and he put her in the seat in front of me and strapped her in. "This is the driver of the vehicle. A tyre burst, and she was going too fast, so the car rolled over. She's in total shock and not speaking." Another two people climbed into the car and Marcus set off for the police station.

The rules in Tanzania are that no road traffic accident victim is to be taken to hospital unless a police recorded number is obtained. Consequently, precious time is lost with this action, but I knew that would be where Marcus would be heading first. I looked at the young man laid across my knees and guessed he would be about 19-20 years of age. He was pretty cut up on his face, his eyes were fixed on mine, when, unexpectedly, he lent forward and coughed up a lot of blood which went all over me. The woman who had part of the young man sitting across her legs "started the 'women's wail of danger," which is a high pitched "whooeeewhoooeee" which signals to people that this woman needs help. I asked the women quite calmly to "be quiet or she would be put out the of the car" as I was not going to be disturbed by all this noise, and I knew it would frighten the injured man. She stopped immediately. We pulled in to the local police station, and Marcus dashed into the station coming out shortly with three police officers. I have to admit they were pretty quick in giving us the number when they saw me and the guy covered in blood. The officers wanted to know which hospital we were going to take the accident victims too, and we said the main hospital which was thirty kilometers away. With lights full on and the horn blaring out at regular intervals, Marcus put his foot down on the accelerator to get to the hospital hopefully in time to save this young man's life as he obviously had serious internal injuries. During the journey, this young man twice coughed up more blood as he reached forward to cough it out, I was now in a pretty bad mess. I considered that my latex gloves were pretty useless now, and I hoped to God he wasn't carrying the HIV/AIDS virus.

We arrived at the hospital casualty department, and Marcus once again jumped out of the vehicle to go fetch a gurney/stretcher. He came back with two doctors and an orderly, and they carefully extracted the young man out of the rear of the vehicle. The young woman driver who had not said a word during the journey was helped out and taken into casualty also. I watched from the back seat as they wheeled the young man away, and I prayed for him. During the whole journey, he had never taken his eyes from me as I stroked his hand and prayed for him. After a few moments of sitting and praying, I got up and left the vehicle.

People were sitting outside the hospital casualty department, and I could see their faces as they looked at this wazungu (European) lean against the vehicle covered in blood. The gloves had been pretty useless after all, and I started to remove them. The blood had sprayed all up my arms and down my skirt and blouse. I was still leaning against the vehicle, when a hospital orderly came up to me with a bowl of cold water. "Wash yourself," he instructed as he held out the bowl to me. Just at that moment, it became a Holy moment, when I had this deep sense of peace and calm wash over me as I looked at this man holding the bowl of water out towards me in an act of great kindness, and it was as if Jesus himself was there with me, not to wash my feet, but to wash my hands. I gently dipped both my arms into the cold water up to my elbows and watched as the water changed colour, and that precious moment was gone. I withdrew my arms, and the man took the bloodied water away. Once again, I leaned against the vehicle, my arms and hands quickly drying in the heat of the sun, and I heard Marcus shouting to me from the top of the ramp and waving his arms in the air in an excited fashion. "Mum! Mum! Isn't God absolutely amazing?" he shouted as he started down the ramp towards me. "Can you believe what has just happened? Isn't He just Amazing !?", he repeated. He had now reached my side and for some reason was just 'buzzing' as he looked at my bewildered face. "Mum? Don't you get it!" he said impatiently, "God just knew no-one would stop to help those people today because no-one would take a bleeding person in their car as they would make such a mess of it." I took a quick glance at the back seat where all the drama had played out and saw that it was in a real mess. He helped me into the passenger seat, and strapped me in, still thrilled about how 'Great is our God' and how he had used us to help these people, and that's why he was late picking everybody up because today we were the transport needed in God's plan. I sat and marveled at my son and wondered how on earth I had got to be so blessed to have him here in Tanzania with me helping with God's mission.

CHAPTER FORTY-ONE
A MIRACLE ON CAMERA

Driving back from the mines, my mobile phone rang, and it was Coupa on the other end of the phone asking me to hurry back to the White House. "Why?" I respond. "What's the drama for today?" "Only that there is an ambulance parked outside the door with two seriously sick children in it. The hospital social worker is requesting that we take care of them, and they really do look serious. They're just little skeletons." "If they are that sick do they have the virus?" I asked. "Yes. The mother is in hospital not expected to live, and the father is unknown at this stage." "On reflection, the hospital has probably sent them to us for some TLC before they pass over. Ensure all the formalities have been completed and ring for the doctor to come and check them over please. It will take me another forty minutes before I reach you. Have the kettle on the boil. It looks as if the day is going to be another long one."

There was not an ounce of meat on the pair, just skin and bone, and they were both too weak even to stand or walk. They were placed in the nursery, and we honestly did not have much hope for their survival. But unbelievably, against all odds, and with the credit due to the loving care of our staff, and the prayers that we interceded for the children they started to pull around and gain weight. Our visitors could not believe the change that was taking place with them from week to week . My greatest joy was when I walked both children in to see the hospital doctor who had sent them to LIA. When she saw them, she threw her hands in the air and shouted, "Mungu Wangu," (My God) then came over and gave each child a hug. Five years later, the little girl has grown taller than her brother and has 'stacked' some weight on, and no one would ever guess the condition she had been in when she arrived at Light in Africa.

A couple of years ago, Lee Harding, a regular volunteer from Iowa, USA, and Mark Anderson and Nina Bouphasavanh from Minneapolis came over to visit with us. Whilst eating a 'hearty' breakfast of pancakes with syrup and fruits and discussing the forthcoming dispensary we were going to hold in a remote region of Maasailand, when Frank, our youth pastor came up the dining room steps two at a time and shouted, "Quick! Everyone in the car! We have an emergency at Pilgrims!" We dashed out, as Mark grabbed his camera, and we ran to the vehicle. A Light in Africa nurse just happened to be passing by, was hauled into the vehicle, and we sped off to the boy's home. As we screeched to a halt, a carer was outside of the home holding a child in her arms who was either fast asleep or unconscious by the way the child's head was and body was hanging loose. The child was handed to the nurse as the sliding door was firmly closed and a three point turn was quickly negotiated. "What's the story?" "What did the carer say had happened?" I asked. "His class teacher thought the child had fallen asleep at his desk and didn't disturb him until the break time only to find when she tried to rouse him he wouldn't wake up. She ran all the way to the home. That's when our carer rang us." "Which hospital are we going to"? shouted Pastor as I noticed the speedometer had already reached 100 k. "We don't have time to go to Moshi. The child is dying," I said. "We shall have to take him to our local district hospital." The vehicle screeched to a resounding halt outside the out-patients clinic as the driver jumped out of the car to let everyone out of the rear of the mini-bus. Nurse was out first and running into the hospital holding tightly to the child. She was a familiar face at the hospital, and with LIA caring for so many children, inevitably there was always a child needing some sort of medical care, and our volunteers who were over for their medical electives would spend time here accompanying the doctors on the wards. Without so much as a knock on the door, nurse pushed the door open into the doctor's surgery, quickly followed by our group. She was explaining to the doctor the course of the events when she went over to the examination table and laid the child down.

The doctor asked the patient he was seeing if he would kindly leave the room and wait in the waiting room, as he went over with his stethoscope to listen to the child's heartbeat and take his pulse. Hospital nurses had now come into the room and the doctor gave instructions to them to hurry and prepare an IV. The doctor repeatedly tried to insert a needle into the boy's right arm, but it was of no use, his veins had already collapsed. The doctor pulled the table away from the window which would allow him access to the boy's left arm. There were more attempts to get the needle in but the child's life was ebbing away. The nurse made a grab for a chair to sit Nina on it before she collapsed, and Lee was already emotional at the thought of the child dying. I was stood against the wall, and Mark was to the left of me filming the events as they took place.

As I had my hands behind my back touching the wall, and praying for the recovery of this child. I sensed in my spirit that I had to go over and whisper to the child "Jesus loves you," I went over to where he lay and whispered in his ear, "Bum bum bum, Jesus loves you." As I patted the left side of his face, I again said, "bum bum bum, Jesus loves you," and I kept saying the same sentence over and over again, according to Mark, for eight minutes. I felt such power spreading up my left arm. It almost felt as if I could throw out thunderbolts as I patted the child's face, and then suddenly he opened his eyes. As I looked at him I could see his right eye had a glazing starting to cover his eye, then the doctor moved in on the child, and I moved back and burst into tears. The child spent five days in hospital recovering.

Mark had shot some more film for "Ten Days in the Life of 'Light In Africa', and on his return to the USA, he edited it with Nina and made a DVD. The name for the DVD that was chosen was "The Angel of Kilimanjaro." When we travelled to Moshi, and I got out of the vehicle, the first person who spots me is the father of one of our children. He opened his arm and proclaimed, "Ah, the Angel of Kilimanjaro." We started to walk down the street, and another friend we know exclaimed the same sentence, and by the time we entered Dot Café, which is the internet service that I use, Nictesh repeats the same sentence, so that is how the title on the DVD came about. Mark entered the DVD in to a film festival, and it won a "Telly" award. As for the child, he is fine, and both he and his sister live at Tudor Village.

CHAPTER FORTY-TWO
SENSELESS BRAVERY

It was a Sunday morning at Tudor Village which is the home for around 100 girls. The children had listened carefully to the service, as for the umpteenth time, I had re-enacted the story of David and Goliath. Whenever I would dramatically pull out the sword from the scabbard to chop off the head of Goliath, the little tots would all push back on their bottoms to get away from the sweep of my arm that they knew was coming, and when I brought my arm down little squeals would emit from them as the bad giant had been disposed of. Whenever I asked, "Which story shall we tell today?" it was always the same one: the story of David and Goliath, the drama of a young boy who God had called and with just five pebbles had brought the bad giant crashing down and saved the Israelite nation.

And from this little drama, I would give a life lesson, which I had heard preached to me.

> What you see, will make you flee
>
> What you hear will make you fear,
>
> But what you know will make you go.

(1 Samuel 17:4-51) NIV Study Bible - The Israelite army saw this fearful looking nine foot giant of a man, who, by his size and the armour that he wore, looked terrifying. What you see will make you flee. Goliath stood and shouted to the ranks of Israel, "Why do you

come out and line up for battle? Am I not a Philistine, and are you not a servant of Saul? Choose a man and have him come down to me. If he is able to fight and kill me, we will become your subjects; but if I overcome him and kill him, you will become our subjects and serve us." Then the Philistine said, "This day I defy the ranks of Israel! Give me a man and let us fight each other." (24) When the Israelite saw the man, they all ran from him in great fear. What you hear will make you fear. On hearing the Philistines words, Saul and all the Israelites were dismayed and terrified. But what you know will make you go. (37) "The Lord who delivered me from the paw of the lion and the paw of the bear will deliver me from the hand of this Philistine" said the young boy David. And of course the Lord fulfilled David's faith in Him.

I was walking away from the home with my hands being clutched by many children, when I saw a bicycle racing towards me at a fast speed and it screeched to a halt beside of me. It was the security guard from the boy's home which was situated just five minutes away and housed the boy's from seven years upwards. He jumped off his bike and told me to go quickly to the home. He kept repeating the words "hatari sana, hatari sana", which means "very dangerous." I ran over to the car park, jumped into my car, and rushed down the mud track to the boy's home. There, standing outside the gate, a large crowd had gathered, and as I approached, our mini-bus dashed out the gate with my son Marcus driving the vehicle. He didn't even stop to tell me what the problem was. He just put his foot down on the accelerator and was gone.

I saw his wife standing on the path looking at the departing vehicle, and I pulled in to the yard and switched off the car engine. "What's happened?" I asked. "Why are all these people at the gate? What are they staring at?" "Oh, mum. It's been terrible!" she said emotionally. "One of the boys spotted a wasp's nest under the roof eaves, and he threw a stone at it. The wasps all began to swarm over all the children playing outside. The staff managed to get all the children inside and shut the doors and close the windows, but they left poor Roger outside on the grass, (Roger has cerebral palsy and is unable to walk) and the wasps swarmed and covered him and stung him all over. The staff called us from inside the house to come and help him so we dashed over. Marcus saw the boy covered in wasps and rushed over to him. He attracted the wasps attention by waving his hands in the air, and then they swarmed and attacked him. He waited, being stung all the time until he had the crowd of wasps around him, and then he ran into the maize and started to throw soil into the air so the wasps couldn't fly. Then they dropped to the floor where he stamped on them. There were still a lot of wasps on Roger, and I suddenly had this idea of spraying him with insect repellent all over, but mum he is so badly stung! His face has swollen like a balloon. Marcus has just taken him to the local hospital because we don't know if he is going to make it. At this comment she burst into tears.

The staff were now coming out of the home and came to comfort Gudilla. I got back into the car and reversed out the gate where there was still a large crowd gathered, I felt hostile towards them for not going to help the staff or the child because I knew they just wanted to see the drama acted out. I reached the hospital, and four doctors were already in the process of removing all the stings while Roger was unconscious. Two hours later, they put him in the ambulance and transferred him to the large hospital in Moshi, where he was immediately placed in intensive care for five days. He was totally unrecognizable. He then was returned to Pilgrim House which has been his home for the last seven years.

Marcus too was badly stung and had to be injected and the stings removed before he was discharged from hospital.

We perhaps often wonder how anyone of us is going to re-act in an emergency. I don't think Marcus need concern himself with that thought, as he already knows.

The sermon that I had preached just an hour earlier had the same connotations as Marcus had to face. He SAW a swarm of wasps covering a disabled child, and his compassion for the child lying on the grass covered in wasps overcame his concern for himself. He waited, and HEARD the wasps buzzing around him and stinging him until they had all swarmed on him, and he was able to take the swarm away from the child. And with the faith that he has, he KNEW he was in God's hands.

CHAPTER FORTY-THREE

ANNA

O ver the last nine years that we have operated two children's homes and a daily food kitchen in a mining area of Tanzania, visitors to our centers are sometimes 'shocked' at the austerity of the area. Although classed as a town, it has no banks or post offices, due partially to the criminal element living in the area. As one visitor put it: "I have travelled the world and I have witnessed poverty, but nothing like the 'hopeless' poverty that exists in this place." Each year when the 'rains' arrive, houses built of mud bricks collapse and damage the occupants of the home. They then become homeless, and the children wander the streets until it is time to visit our food kitchen. Often we can have a whole family of six to eight children attending because there is no food to eat at their home, and this is the only meal that they can reckon on for the whole day. It is seeing the little five or six year old girls who arrive for food carrying their little brother or sister in a kanga (material) on their backs, and seeing them sit down on a platform bench and start to spoon feed the little tots that gets to one's emotions the most.

But poverty is not the only problem of the area. There is also no clean drinking water. There is plenty of water when we dig to the water level, but it contains such high concentrates of fluoride it is quite undrinkable. If you are poor, there is no way that you can purchase even a cup or a bucket of clean drinking water from the many lorries that travel the twenty kilometers each day to replenish their supplies of clean water to enable them to distribute to the local people. LIA has to purchase this water from the lorries each day for the homes and the food kitchen at a highly inflated price. People living in and around the rural areas have no chance to purchase this clean water, and are subjected to drinking 'well water' which usually has a layer of grease floating on the top of it. For children and babies being given this water to drink, it has drastic consequences on their health.

Through our medical out-reach programs into the rural areas of the bush, we see children being brought to us with severely distorted and twisted legs due to all the fluoride that damages soft bones, with no hope of gaining an education as they are unable to walk the distance to the school. Over the years, through the kindness and generosity of our volunteers who are so touched by the plight of these children, we have been able to help many children receive operations to have their legs 'straightened' and be able to walk straight and attend school.

At one of our dispensaries in a remote Maasai village, we were brought a young ten-year-old Maasai girl with such distorted legs it took the surgeons six breaks on each leg to get them straightened out. She was returned to her village after rehabilitation only for us to find that now that she had straight legs her parents thought that they could receive a dowry for her and word was out that she was now available to marry. With the help of our Maasai chairman, she was brought back to our facility where she has lived with us ever since. (see before and after pictures)

Doctors from overseas, who organize medical missions abroad, contact me to ask if they can contribute to our organization by flying over a medical orthopaedic team to perform operations on our or other children at our local hospital. To this, I readily agree.

A doctor, who is a senior Orthopaedic surgeon at a large children's hospital in California, asked if I could arrange for children with disabilities to be made available for him to assess on just a short three day trip to Tanzania before flying over a medical team later on.

'Bush Telegraph' is amazing, and as long as I can give three weeks' notice for word to penetrate through the bush, I knew children would be brought to see the doctor before being bussed to the hospital for X-rays to be taken. The doctor would then return to his country to show his colleagues, the sort of operations that would be required on the children.

Security opened the gates for the first arrivals. A young Maasai youth of about seventeen years who 'dragged' his leg along as he walked was the first patient to be seen by the doctor. After a thorough examination, he went off to our kitchen to eat some food as he had no breakfast that morning whilst the doctor examined more patients.

Our attention was then drawn to a small man carrying a girl on his back. He gasped for breath as he sat her down on the bench outside, and we could then see that the girl of around fifteen years was unable to walk as she had just two very small legs which she dragged behind her as she walked upon her knees. The girl's father had been prepared to carry his daughter for 3 kilometers on his back just for the chance for her to see a doctor 'free' of charge. The doctor was somewhat taken aback when the girl's father took one of my hands in his and spat in to the palm. I always send up a quick arrow prayer when the older people do this to me as a traditional mark of respect: "Dear God I pray for protection that this man isn't carrying the TB or cholera virus" and I quickly excuse myself to enable me to wash my hands and apply antibacterial solutions. This is one tradition that I hope will soon be exterminated.

When all the examinations had been completed, we made our way to the hospital for consultations and X-rays. By the end of the day, the visiting doctor thought that it would be best for Anna if she could travel to his hospital in the USA and have a double amputation on both her legs and have prosthetics made to allow her to "walk tall."

It was to take a further eighteen months before a visa for her was eventually obtained, but it was not without overcoming many difficulties.

With her father being a peasant farmer, and never having travelled from outside his village before, difficulties arose in gaining the necessary paper work before the Embassy was able to issue the visa. The father was required to go to Dar es Salaam to have a lawyer compose paper work which said he was Anna's father and that he gave permission for the hospital to perform the operation, and then visit the Tanzanian Immigration Department for permission for Anna to leave the country. As I was already in Dar es Salaam, our youth Pastor agreed to accompany Anna and her father on the coach to Dar. As the coach approached, the father was seen to back away and become very fearful, and for a moment, the Pastor thought that he might change his mind and run away. "The coach is so big," he said as it pulled to a stop beside them for them to board. With encouragement from the Pastor and seeing his daughter being carried up the steps to her assigned seat, he nervously ventured up the steps of the coach and sat down. Allowances were made for the journey which should have taken around 8 hours, so an appointment was made at the lawyer's office for 6:00 p. m. for all the necessary papers to be signed. At 6:00 p. m., they were still sitting on the coach after numerous breakdowns. Frantic phone calls were made to the lawyer, and he very kindly agreed to wait at his office until they arrived. I met up with them when the coach arrived, and it was 8:00 p. m. in the evening before the papers were all signed. The following day, we were back at the lawyer's office to collect more official paper work that was requested by the Immigration Dept. The lawyer walked us out of his office to the lifts which would take us down from the fifth to the ground floor. With Anna being 'piggy backed' by the Pastor, the lift arrived, and we all squeezed in. It started to descend, and then quite suddenly, the lift started to shudder, then stop, and then the lights went out which left us trapped in the dark inside the lift. Now, as my mother had broken her back by falling down a lift shaft, being stuck in the dark in one was not a comfortable thought for me. My only solace before panic set in was to pray silently for a quick rescue. As Anna had no idea of the mechanics or consequences of a lift failure she was quite convinced that soon it would start up again and sat patiently waiting on the lift floor.

But not so our present companions stuck in the lift with us as they started banging on the lift doors and shouting for help. Twenty minutes passed and perspiration was flowing down our bodies from being confined in such a small space, before we heard voices and a crack of light appeared between the doors. Another problem that soon became apparent was that we were stuck between the floors. The door was cracked open and people stood glaring down at us from above. A distance of over 5' had to be managed before we could reach the safety of the floor. Men started to kneel on the floor and offer down their hands whilst the men in the lift cupped hands together for the women to stand on, and one by one we were brought to safety. Two men had to hold Anna up whilst willing hands grabbed hold of her and sat her safely down on the concrete floor. I just thanked God that her father had decided to stay at the hotel instead of accompanying us to the lawyer's office. Had he been there, the outcome of this little drama might have been somewhat different.

We arrived in America on a Saturday, and the operation was scheduled for the following Tuesday which gave the doctor just one working day to have all the necessary tests and procedures completed. The first port of call was to have an appointment with a geneticist who traced the cause of her disability. She was given some disturbing news which made her cry. We then moved off for an appointment at the heart specialists', who diagnosed that Anna had a heart murmur. Thrown into a fluster that the operation would not now go ahead and we had travelled all this distance unnecessarily, I sat and waited patiently in the reception area whilst more tests were completed on Anna's heart. The heart specialist eventually appeared and said "We're good to go," and the amputation to remove both Anna's legs went ahead the following day.

Her stay in 'intensive care' was not without its problems for the pain management team. Tanzanians, it seems, have a higher threshold for pain than Europeans, (I have only to think of my daughter-in-law who will have a tooth pulled out while just sitting on a wooden chair with her head held against the wall for leverage) and only when the pain was extreme would she cry out. She also had a reaction from the morphine drug so alternatives had to be found for the duration of her hospital stay.

During her time in America, Anna had an awful lot of fuss made of her. She had interviews with the local press and videos made of her before and after her operation. An appointment book had to be made with all the wonderful Californian people wanting to share her happiness and showering her with lovely gifts. The gentleman who was making Anna's prosthetic legs invited us along with his family to visit Disneyland which was a wonderment in itself for her. As she sat on a horse riding around on a carousel, purchasing Mickey Mouse ears, and going on a boat trip for the very first time, her persona took on a new identity. Every morning, Anna would now take great care in painting her nails and putting on the new dresses that had been bought for her, and Justin Bieber became the man of her dreams and she could not get enough of watching the TV screen although she did not understand a word of what was being said. Physiotherapy was grueling for her, and it was going to take quite some time before one of her legs was going to heal sufficiently for her to wear her pros-thetics, so I made the decision for this African young girl who had undergone a metamorphoses to be returned to her own country and continue the treatment at Tudor Village with our own nurse.

Anna is now proudly walking on her 'new legs' and is quite happy to pose for photos for the many visitors who arrive at Tudor Village.

Anna is attending an interview shortly for a place at a rehabilita-tion center where she will then decide on a choice of career for her future.

CHAPTER FORTY-FOUR
TORCHBEARER CO. LTD -
A FAMILY BUSINESS

Whilst I was in Nairobi with Tuesday, the very sick little Maasai boy who we had a referral letter from a hospital which diagnosed that the child was suffering from cancer leukemia, and whilst waiting for his pathology results to come through, I ended up with an afternoon free. I laid on my bed at the hostel, and my mind started wondering about all the children in our care. With employment being so scarce, how could I possibly stop them returning to the streets and back into the downward poverty spiral?

The ones who were academic and well educated would of course stand a lot better chance than the children who had had very little education of gaining meaningful employment. I thought of one child in particular who, up to the age of nine, had had very limited education. As the oldest child she had to care for her younger siblings whilst her mother worked both night and day shifts. How could I possibly ensure that she had a job to go to? Then there was the young teenager who, although well-built and able to accomplish some menial work, had a mental disability and would need to be in 'sheltered accommodation' for her own protection. How could I ensure her future was one of fulfillment where she could be empowered to enable her to enjoy a weekly wage? My mind wouldn't let go of all these scenarios.

With thirty children leaving secondary school in one year, what could I possibly do to help them? Most people, when they have things on their mind, find it very difficult to "let it go", it was the same with me and this idea of "what am I going to do for the children's future?" it became quite persistent.

By the time our little Maasai group returned to Tudor Village with the wonderful news that Tuesday did not have cancer, I had formed an idea that I needed to share with the Executive Committee of Light in Africa on our return.

With two of our Executive members becoming Directors of a Limited Company, we could ensure that the 'for profit' company would be able to provide training and life skills to our children as well as with any profits make donations to Light in Africa Children's Home's towards their running costs. To date, five quality guest houses have been constructed amongst fruit trees of papaya and pomegranates and exotic flowers. The view of Mount Kilimanjaro from our outside patio is captivating on a cloudless day whilst enjoying a cold beverage. Our Secondary School leavers give a mandatory twelve months of service back to LIA, and they learn all the aspects of providing accommodation to our tourists and volunteers, from front desk reception, to business management, catering, IT, safari guiding, caring for the environment, and all the other 'every day' occurrences which ensure our guests are provided with a quality service. As Tudor Village is just twenty minutes away from the International Airport, visitors can be collected with our airport taxi service and easily brought to our accommodation rather travelling a further hour after a long flight to either Moshi or Arusha the nearest town or city.

For our students who require assisted living and support, we are opening on our four acre site a Butterfly and Lavender farm. This venture is a poverty reduction initiative which will help the teenagers to manage the butterfly farm and grow the lavender which will then be made into soaps, moisturizing cream, and also lavender biscuits and other commodities which will all be sold on our on-site shop. We are hoping this venture will be completed and open by December 2014. Already over 2,000 lavender cuttings have been grown and planted by the students, and each Sunday morning, different groups, both boys and girls, enter the Domestic Science room and bake 150 buns and cakes for the afternoon children's service, as well as learning skills from sewing a button on to growing vegetables, planting trees, making cement pathways, rug making, sewing, knitting, crochet, and quilting.

The most exciting idea, I think, which came from the Nairobi trip, was when I was thinking about our Maasai friends, and how could I possibly help them and their families with the very special relationship that we have with the tribe. It was then I came up with the idea of an Extreme Maasai Wilderness Survival Experience, where by working together, we could offer to our volunteers and guests the opportunity of a life-time to live, walk, and learn the survival skills of the Maasai over a ninety seven kilometer walk with the donkeys and cattle. This unique opportunity, which is only available because LIA has been working with the Kilimanjaro Maasai for over twelve years, has been a resounding success. Everyone who has walked the 3-5 day trek has come away with a deeper understanding of natural life from learning to light a fire with two sticks (One guest didn't believe he could do it. He thought it was just a myth!) to learning about the medicine trees that the Maasai use for treatments to cooking and roasting meat on a spit, under the stars. Both men and women have committed to this most-unusual and exciting challenge which is available to anyone over the age of eighteen years.

Light in Africa continues to welcome volunteers who wish to support and work with our community programs, and now through TorchBearer, the everyday tourist can enjoy the natural resources of Tanzania (safari in our national parks and climb Mt. Kilimanjaro) and know that their travel dollars go towards supporting a worthy cause, and enabling our children to gain valuable work skills.

With these new idea's being put into action, I feel happier about the future for our many children whose lives have been saved because I dared to follow a voice which said, "GO TO AFRICA."

ACKNOWLEDGEMENTS

After two and a half years working with the 'lost' children of Kilimanjaro -as the Maasai refer to them- I returned to my home town in Lincolnshire in the UK to visit my family. Whilst there I was posed a very deep meaningful question by a friend, who asked: "Lynn, I don't want to be disrespectful to you but why did God choose you?" At that time, I was lost for words but mumbled something like, perhaps God had ask other believers to go to Africa but they were not prepared to leave everything behind that they loved, to go and live in a strange country and follow 'The Way.' On my return to Tanzania, I prayed deeply about this question. "God, why did you choose such an un-deserving person as me to do your work in Africa?" I arose from my knees and walked over to my bookshelf, randomly choosing a book, and, opened it somewhere in the middle. The title of the chapter was 'God doesn't choose the qualified, but qualifies the Chosen.'

The people who are mentioned below have all accepted me- just as God did – with all of my flaws and 'quirky' British behavior, and for that I am deeply grateful to them.

Firstly, my friends I return to on my visits back home where I know there will be fish and chips and a pot of tea awaiting my arrival. Chris, Mel and Paul, and Miriam, Andy and Karen, Carol, John and Pastor

Graham Jamson, who very kindly operates our UK bank accounts. Mr. 'Enigma', Roger and Roy, three of the best. Mary & Brian Clark, who each year swim in the cold waters of the lake district and hold coffee mornings to raise funds for our children. Dr. Rachael Taylor/Ben and Alex. What can I say to express our appreciation? Only God knows.

For The Executive Committee of Light in Africa who handle all the day to day management of the centers: Thank you for your 24 hr a day commitment to our children. To the local agencies of the Police, the Gender Violence Team, Social Welfare Officers: together in partnership we can make a real difference to the lives of children, and we can be true advocates of Justice. Thank you for your commitment to our children. All of our staff who works so hard ensuring our children are well cared for and loved, it doesn't go unnoticed. A special mention and a "thank you" to my right hand mama Coupa, who I named after a Datsun car I owned which never let me down, you are a 'standard bearer' for your people. For Manure: handling a very difficult job in the mining area with such ease, thank you. For mama Queenie working in the 'special needs' unit: you inspire me with your courage. For the first friends that I met on arrival in the country, Shafiq and Muntaz Kanji of Emslies Global Travel who rescue me from different parts of the world when I need to urgently return home. To the family at Dot Café -- Dorothy, Dishant, Nitesh, Anita, Bhavna, Karan, Dyutit, Vanishka, and Vivaan -- your patience with my computer illiteracy put's Job to shame. Mama Shazma and Mr. & Mrs. Doudi who the children love to love. Thank you.

For the two Paul's in my life, our webmaster and his wife Lily in Holland, and the General Manager of Torchbearer, your organizing abilities amaze me.

For Dr. Minja and Dr. Richard, you both deserve gold medals as big as dustbin lids for the work you do amongst your people, never ever turning a patient away if they have no money to pay for treatment. You are my heroes. For our administrators in Germany, Linda and Josephine, Wilfred, and in Holland, Marijke and Jonathan, who just can't seem to get enough of our children and keep coming back. In the USA, Joan & Mark Coleman (whose sands of Africa is between your feet so you just have to keep returning). I have a chance now to personally thank Dr.Tai S. Kim for the eye surgery that he performed, and Dr. Whirta who didn't 'sugar coat' the diagnoses, and his lovely wife who showed me such care and compassion. For Dr. Afshin Amenium and his medical team for the surgery that you performed on Anna's legs. With grateful thanks to Lauren and his family who made such an excellent job of making Anna's new prosthetic legs, you have indeed changed her life from one of knees to "walking tall." Thank you. Sara & Abigail, Lee & Nicole Harding and the children where I just love the peace and quiet of your basement, Don and Debbie. With a special mention to Pastor Jean and for Elizabeth & Steven Wilcox; Marcus still remembers his Harley Davidson ride! And the farming community of Iowa. For Marylin in Sioux City and Sue. For Dennis and Sherry from Texas who gave so unstintingly to our needs in the early days. To our friends in Malibu Jim & Cindy, Rose & Phil and the congregation of Malibu Pres. who made Tudor Village possible.

To Tony from Long Beach, who saved a child's life because of his insistant persistance. Bless You.

To Jessica T – bless you, and Arlene who makes my heart sing when I listen to you play the piano.

To Kelly, who is holding my hand whilst I walk down this unchartered path of becoming an author, thank you friend. To Sammye who lives down the road from me and is the most multi-faceted person that I have ever known. No sooner is it said, then it is done. Thank you for your help Sammye in compiling this book.

And to Justin Sachs of Motivational Press, thank you for allowing me to join your family.

Last, but certainly by no means least, are the two thousand odd volunteers who have travelled over to Africa from all parts of the world to help out with our children and make a difference to the lives of the poor. We salute you.

To all of our friends who sponsor our children throughout the years and our friends who go through extreme initiation ceremonies like the men having their legs waxed to raise money for us. Ouch!!!! To Manfred & his wife, who always remember us although we live so far away.

Although I have used words to write this book, they just seem so inadequate when it comes to thanking everyone who has helped to make Light in Africa a beacon in this area of child care in Tanzania. May the light of God shine brightly in your lives.

Mama Lynn and her son Marcus still live in Tanzania helping with the mission of Light in Africa's Children's Homes.

If you should wish to visit the children at Tudor Village, Boman'gnombe, Tanzania (near Kilimanjaro International Airport) please visit our website at www.lightinafrica.org or email us at

africa@lightinafrica.org

If you should wish to stay at Torchbearer Co. Ltd., (Family Business) accommodation then please make reservation through info@ torch-bearer.com where your enquiries will be quickly responded to.

Thank you.